in the BUSH

PM Leary
MD SCP(SA) DCH

STRUIK

Struik Publishers (Pty) Ltd
(a member of The Struik Publishing Group (Pty) Ltd)
Cornelis Struik House
80 McKenzie Street
Cape Town
8001

Reg. No. 54/00965/07

First published in 1994
Second impression 1997

Editor: Hilda Hermann
Illustrator: Theo Hawkins, Inkspiration Graphics
Designer: Peter Bosman

Reproduction by cmyk pre-press, Cape Town
Printed and bound by CTP Book Printers (Pty) Ltd,
Caxton Street, Parow, Cape Town

ISBN 1 86825 457 7

CONTENTS

Introduction 4
About the Author 5
Planning and Preparation 6
Composition of the Party 6
Route Planning 7
Weather 8
Clothing, Equipment and Food 8
Survival Kits 13
How to Handle an Accident 14
Examination of an Injured Person 15
Moving an Injured Person 18
First Aid Kits 19
Leadership and Morale 21
Finding the Way 22
Setting Up Camp 25
Mountain Safety Guidelines 29
Improvising Shelter 31
Lightning Strikes 33
Fire 34
River Crossing 37
Rescuing a Drowning Person 39
Use of a Radio 41

A–Z of Outdoor First Aid
and Medical Emergencies 43

Useful Addresses 138
Poison Centres 139
Further Reading 140
Index 141

INTRODUCTION

The founder of the Scout movement, Lord Baden-Powell, spent much of his life living out-of-doors in places remote from the amenities of cities and towns. His experience led him to suggest as a motto for scouts the phrase: 'Be Prepared'. This advice applies to mountaineers, hikers and trail walkers as much today as it did in Baden-Powell's time.

Maximum enjoyment of an expedition, climb or walk will be achieved only if preparations have been thorough, and survival in an emergency may well depend on the training and preparedness of those involved.

This book is directed at the inexperienced hiker who wishes to plan outings in a sensible manner and have available the information necessary to deal with emergency situations. It is neither a comprehensive manual on outdoor living nor a medical textbook. Readers will find guidelines on planning an excursion, advice about direction finding, map reading and camping, lists of appropriate responses in hazardous circumstances and essential information about a wide range of medical conditions. Cross references at the end of certain sections draw attention to other relevant information.

The book has been written with a view to easy reading while planning any expedition and for ready reference during the course of a hike. It is designed to fit easily into the side pocket of a backpack.

Those who seek recreation and pleasure in the mountains, on cross-country expeditions and along hiking trails will find useful information in this book. Being aware of potential hazards and having some knowledge of first aid and its application, together with good camping technique, will go a long way towards ensuring that every outing is enjoyable and that all return home safely.

About the Author

Professor Mick Leary has lived in Cape Town for much of his life. He is a paediatrician on the staff of the Red Cross Children's Hospital and an associate professor in the Department of Paediatrics and Child Health at the University of Cape Town. His early camping and climbing experience was obtained as a member of a scout troop. Since his undergraduate days he has been an active member of the Mountain Club of South Africa and he has served on the club's Search and Rescue Committee for many years.

PLANNING AND PREPARATION

The desire to undertake a particular hike, climb, trail or expedition may arise in various ways. You may read about it in a guide book, journal or travelogue. Friends who have done the trip may give an enthusiastic report. Your curiosity may be aroused when studying a map, or, the oldest reason of all, you may want to do the trip because you have an adventurous nature and the mountain or cross-country route *is there*. Whatever the stimulus, careful planning is essential if the trip is to be completed safely and enjoyed by all.

COMPOSITION OF THE PARTY

The number of people in a party will obviously vary. However, there should be at least four people on mountain climbs and hiking trails so that two can go for help if an emergency arises. Parties in excess of 20 are difficult for one leader to control.

The age distribution of party members also merits some consideration. In general, greatest compatibility is achieved when members are all in the same broad age group. However, with sound and considerate leadership (for example, a slower pace to accommodate older members), parties encompassing a wide age spectrum can function very well. When children are included, careful attention must be given to their special needs with regard to over-exertion, fluid intake and protection from the elements.

All members of the party should be fit enough to meet the physical demands of the planned excursion.

It is most inadvisable to set off on a demanding climb or hike when some members are not in good physical condition, and a number of preliminary, shorter 'get fit' outings should be undertaken. These will also serve to identify deficiencies in boots, clothing and other equipment. A hiker on regular medication (for example, for asthma, blood pressure or diabetes), should carry a supply sufficient to cater for his or her personal needs during the planned trip and a little extra in reserve.

When embarking on a major expedition to a remote area, it is highly advisable to include in the party a doctor, nursing sister or someone with practical first aid training. Responsibility for the health care of the party should be delegated to this person, who must be capable of setting up an intravenous infusion and administering strong, pain-killing drugs.

ROUTE PLANNING

To plan the route effectively, a goal must be defined and information obtained about the terrain to be traversed. The best source for information is an experienced hiker who has done the trip before and can provide details about the state of paths, availability of water, the nature of vegetation, steepness of mountain slopes and distances between camping spots. This person would be the obvious choice for trail guide if he or she is undertaking the expedition for a second time. If you do not know someone who has the necessary experience, obtain as much information as possible from guide books and detailed maps of the area.

Route planning should take into consideration access roads, paths, gradients, water courses, projected overnight campsites and the distance to be covered each day, bearing in mind the composition of the party. A permit will have to be obtained if State land is to be crossed, and verbal or written permission from a landowner or farmer may be necessary if the projected route crosses private property. Advance booking is required for designated hiking trails.

Before setting out on any climb, hike or expedition, make sure that a responsible person at home knows the composition of the party, the route to be followed, and the estimated time of return. Such information is vital if the party becomes overdue and it is considered necessary to instigate a search and rescue mission. *Do not* deviate from your planned route without very good reason.

Weather

Knowledge about prevailing weather patterns is essential: for example, a hike or climb which is relatively easy and enjoyable in dry, summer weather may become a hazardous ordeal during winter. Conversely, extreme summer heat and water shortage may lead to hyperthermia and death on a hike which is easily accomplished in bracing, winter weather. Thus, both the season of the year and current weather forecast must be considered when making plans. It may be prudent to postpone a planned excursion in the event of adverse weather forecasts.

Clothing, Equipment and Food

These aspects require careful attention during the planning phase of any outing. All three are markedly influenced by the nature and duration of the expedition planned. For a day hike, protective clothing, a survival kit and a small amount of food and water will usually suffice. When an overnight mountain trail is being planned, a stove, cooking utensils, sleeping bag and perhaps a lightweight tent must be carried. On a major, safari-type expedition with motor transport, kitchen equipment, heavy-duty tents, camp beds and a selection of foodstuffs may all be feasible.

CLOTHING

Personal clothing should be comfortable, durable and appropriate for the season and possible weather conditions. Clothing worn while walking should provide adequate protection against the elements: long-sleeved shirts and long shorts will protect against sunburn and scratches while walking through bush. A hat should always be worn. It will protect the head, face and neck from the sun and, in cold conditions will conserve body heat.

Footwear should be appropriate for the terrain anticipated. On mountain climbs and trails, well worn-in boots with non-slip soles are advisable. These should be worn with two pairs of socks: thick wool/nylon socks to cushion the feet and inner cotton socks which will reduce the chance of blisters. Some individuals are happier in sturdy, lightweight sports shoes. These should have non-slip soles of adequate thickness. For boulder-hopping in streams and kloofs lightweight sports shoes are ideal. No hiker should ever venture out on a trail without a sweater, a wind- and waterproof anorak and tracksuit pants. These garments are the minimum requirements for survival in the event of a sudden change in weather, or an unplanned night in the open.

9

A change of clothing will be necessary on extended hikes, trails and expeditions. Only essential items should be carried as each item included adds to the weight of the individual's pack. The checklist below is offered as a guide.

Clothing Checklist

In addition to what is worn take:

Anorak	T-shirt
Waterproof trousers	Underwear
Sweater	Handkerchief
Woollen jacket	Swimming costume
Woollen shirt	Lightweight sport shoes
Long trousers	Hat
(tracksuit)	Socks (wool and cotton)
Gloves	(T-shirt and tracksuit
Shirt	trousers do duty as
Shorts	pyjamas)

EQUIPMENT

For overnight trips, a sleeping bag is essential. This should preferably be down-filled if cold conditions are anticipated. A lightweight, synthetic fibre sleeping bag may suffice in warm, summer conditions.

A lightweight tent will ensure comfortable nights when weather conditions are changeable, and may be life-saving for parties caught in extreme conditions. A wide selection of suitable tents is available – many weigh less than 3 kg and can be carried in a backpack or strapped to one.

Lighting cooking-fires is prohibited in many mountain, wilderness and forestry areas. Furthermore, wood for making a fire is not always available. A small camping stove is an essential item for hikers. Available models burn gas, methylated spirits or benzine. It is important to be familiar with the operation of the stove and to carry enough fuel for the duration of the excursion. Suitable cooking utensils will be required. Useful sets incorporate a small kettle and a lid which does duty as a frying pan. Other items of personal and communal equipment are listed below under 'Equipment Checklist'.

Equipment Checklist

Personal	Communal
Sleeping bag/pillow	Tent
Groundsheet	Stove
Plate, mug, knife, fork and spoon	Fuel
	Cooking pots
Wash kit and small towel	Matches
	Toilet paper
Torch	
Pocket knife	
Survival kit	
Water-bottle	

FOOD

Nowadays, it is seldom possible to 'live off the land'. Game is protected or privately owned, licences must be obtained to hunt and fish, and the picking of fruit or other edible plant matter may well be construed as theft. Therefore, all necessary foodstuffs for the duration of a mountain trail or expedition must be assembled at the start, unless it is feasible to pick up further supplies *en route*.

Quantities of food will depend on the number of people in the party and individual food capacities. When everything is to be carried in backpacks, excessive amounts of sugar, jam, coffee and milk powder should be avoided. All foodstuffs must be packed in watertight, lightweight, plastic containers – tins and glass bottles contribute unnecessary weight.

A practical approach to catering is to set a menu for each meal to be eaten during the course of the

excursion. These menus should take into consideration increased energy expenditure caused by exertion, the limitations of perishable foods, the need to
keep packs as light as possible and the individual
tastes of party members. Good use should be made
of the wide selection of dehydrated milk, meat and
vegetable preparations available. A sample menu for
a three-day mountain traverse is provided below.

Sample Menu

Day 1
Lunch
Pre-packed sandwiches
Apple
Tea or coffee
Supper
Instant soup (packet)
Precooked and frozen
  chicken casserole
  with rice and veget-
  ables (packed in air-
  tight plastic container
  – requires warming)
Yoghurt
Tea or coffee

Day 2
Breakfast
Cereal/muesli/porridge
Bread, margarine, jam
Tea or coffee
Lunch
Sardines on crispbread
Bread and peanut butter
Apple or orange
Tea or coffee

Supper
Instant soup (packet)
Instant soya mince,
  flavoured with onion
  and tomato
Mashed potatoes
  (dehydrated pack)
Vegetables
  (dehydrated pack)
Chocolate mousse
Tea or coffee

Day 3
Breakfast
As for Day 2
Lunch
As for Day 2

Snack foods
Boiled sweets
Rusks
Crystallized fruit
Peanuts
Raisins

The food and communal equipment to be carried should be distributed fairly among party members, taking into consideration individual carrying capacities. Each individual should carry his or her own clothing, sleeping bag, water-bottle and survival kit. The total weight of a backpack should be no more than 25% of the carrier's body weight.

SURVIVAL KITS

Every hiker should carry a 'survival kit'. This may be stored permanently in one of the side pockets of the backpack, and should contain the following:

Reflective space
    blanket
1-2 chocolate-
    coated
    energy bars
250 g peanuts
Pocket torch
Personal first
    aid kit
Signalling mirror

The survival kit is for use in unforeseen and emergency situations, and the foodstuffs should not be 'raided' in the course of an uneventful hike! A space blanket is a sheet of silvered plastic, measuring about 1,2 x 2,4 m. It is so thin that it can be folded into a pocket-sized package. Wrapped round the body in an emergency situation, it will ensure 90% retention of body heat. In dry areas, where water is in short supply, a space blanket can be used to collect dew overnight. A hollow in the ground can be lined with the space blanket and then half filled with stones. Dew will condense on the stones and trickle down to collect at the lowest point (*see* Water, p.27).

HOW TO HANDLE AN ACCIDENT

Accidents happen with dramatic suddenness: a hiker slips on a smooth rock, tumbles and breaks a leg; a climber on a rock-scramble loses his footing, falls backwards and sustains a head injury; a pot of boiling tea is upset over a resting trail walker; during tent-pitching an unwary camper treads on a puff adder and is bitten ... Any one of these unforeseen incidents can convert a pleasant recreational excursion into an emergency situation. The final outcome will depend on the manner in which other members of the party behave.

1 The first concern must be to protect the injured person from further harm. He or she must be removed from fire, lifted out of water or secured on a rock ledge, as the situation demands.

2 The second concern is for the maintenance of vital functions. A clear airway must be established in the unconscious patient (*see* Unconsciousness). Active haemorrhage must be stopped by direct pressure (*see* Bleeding). If there is respiratory and cardiac arrest, artificial respiration and external cardiac massage must be instituted without delay (*see* Artificial Respiration, Heart Attack).

3 When bleeding has been stopped, and respiration and pulse are relatively stable, a brief period of stock-taking and planning is necessary before rescue and evacuation procedures are initiated. Fifteen minutes spent examining the injured patient, making him or her as comfortable as possible and determining the best use of available human and equipment resources, is time well spent. In some instances, injuries may be less serious than at first suspected, and, after a period of rest, the casualty may be able to walk out with the assistance of companions.

4 If urgent medical attention is required, at least one person should remain with the injured individual for comfort and support until rescuers arrive. This person should preferably be the member of the party with greatest knowledge and experience of first aid.

5 Two people should go for help – preferably the fittest and fleetest of foot in the party. In mountainous and unfamiliar terrain, they should take careful note of direction and landmarks so that they can describe accurately to rescuers where the injured person is lying and, if necessary, act as guides for the rescue team.

Accidents should, in the first instance, be reported to the South African Police, who will then notify Metro and other rescue services. Those who report an accident *must* remain at a designated place, for example, the nearest police station, until the rescue team arrives. Details can then be given to the rescue leader and, if necessary, the rescue team can be guided to the scene of the accident.

*E*XAMINATION OF AN INJURED PERSON

The first priority is to establish that:
- The airway is unobstructed;
- Breathing is adequate;
- A pulse can be felt in the neck; and
- There is no active external bleeding.

Immediate steps are necessary to rectify matters if these initial observations reveal abnormality.

■ An attempt should then be made to establish the person's level of consciousness

Next, pay attention to the wrist pulse. Count the rate and assess the quality of each beat. Normal pulse rate at rest in a healthy individual is between 60 and 90 beats. A rapid pulse rate in a conscious individual may be due to anxiety. It will have a strong, full quality. A rapid pulse which is weak and difficult to feel suggests shock or severe pain. If injuries are not obvious suspect internal bleeding. Now carry out a physical examination, starting at the head and working along the body. The injured person should preferably be lying on his or her back, on level ground, with the legs slightly elevated.

HEAD

Note the colour and moistness of the tongue.
A healthy tongue is pink in colour and moist to the touch. Examine the scalp for lacerations and bruising; these may cover an underlying fracture. Note whether there is bleeding or discharge of clear fluid from the ears or nose; this occurs when there has been fracture of the base of the skull. Ascertain whether the injured person can open and shut his or her mouth without discomfort; this is not possible when the jaw has been broken.

See also Bleeding, Face and Nose Injuries, Head Injuries

NECK

Gently palpate the back of the neck and establish whether there is pain or tenderness. Any limitation in movement suggests damage to the cervical spine. The neck should be immobilized immediately with a rolled jersey, backpack waistband or cervical collar (*see* Back and Neck Injuries).

THORAX

Establish whether there is any breathing restriction or pain on inspiration; this suggests rib fractures. Palpate the chest cage gently, noting any points of extreme tenderness. Log roll (*see* Back and Neck Injuries) the person on to one side, and palpate the back and spinal column for tenderness or obvious deformity *(see* Chest Injuries).

ABDOMEN

Encourage the casualty to relax before you feel the surface of the abdomen. Your hands should be warm for this part of the examination.

Tenderness to touch and stiffness of the abdominal wall muscles (guarding) suggests damage to internal organs. Internal haemorrhage is a strong possibility when these signs are present along with pallor, sweating and a weak rapid pulse. In most cases, skilled surgical treatment is urgently needed (*see* Abdominal Injuries).

PELVIS

Palpate over the upper margins of the pelvic bones and hips. In the absence of leg fractures, see if the thighs can be moved without causing pain. Tenderness, deformity and pain on movement suggest fracture or disruption of the pelvis and/or hip dislocation (*see* Dislocated Joints).

LIMBS

Examine the full length of each limb for bruising, lacerations, swelling and deformity. Joint injury causes swelling and limitation of normal movement. Fractures cause deformity of the limb, loss of normal function and extreme pain on any movement. A grating sound (crepitus) may be heard on moving the limb, but this should not be deliberately sought as the pain caused may aggravate shock.

See *also* Fractures.

Moving an Injured Person

Once protected from further injury by falling rocks, fire, immersion etc., the injured person should remain in one place until shock has been treated and an assessment made of the extent of injuries. The airway of an unconscious patient must be continuously monitored. A pain-killing drug should be administered by injection or mouth and, if indicated and feasible, an intravenous infusion should be set up.

Fractured limbs must be immobilized (*see* Fractures), and the neck splinted if there is any suspicion of neck injury. Only when these measures have been taken should the victim be moved.

When placing the patient on a stretcher, use the log rolling technique (*see* Back and Neck Injuries). This requires several helpers and involves rotation of the head and neck, trunk and limbs simultaneously. This manoeuvre prevents the occurrence or aggravation of a spinal cord injury. An alternative technique is for the patient to be lifted horizontally into the air by many helpers while the stretcher is slid into position. Gentleness is the watchword at every step.

Transport by helicopter is undoubtedly the most efficient method of casualty evacuation from a mountain slope or remote wilderness area. When feasible, use may be made of a Paragard stretcher dropped from the helicopter at the site of the accident. The patient is secured in the stretcher and winched up and into the helicopter for a direct flight to hospital, or, if more practicable, suspended below the

helicopter for a
brief flight to a road.

When darkness or
weather conditions preclude the
use of a helicopter, the injured person
will have to be carried on a stretcher.
Mountain rescue teams are equipped with the
Thomas stretcher which has an aluminium frame, a
canvas bed and sturdy wooden runners. It is carried
by a team of ten and can, if necessary, be rigged to
an aerial trapeze or lowered down a rock-face. When
no alternative is available, a stretcher may be improvised with poles, ground sheets, jackets and fynbos.
This is never as effective or comfortable for the casualty as a custom-built stretcher, and should be used
only as a last resort.

FIRST AID KITS

A personal first aid kit should be carried in the survival kit of every hiker, and should contain:

Several Vaseline gauze dressings
A small pack of gauze squares
Plasters of assorted sizes
Betadine
Codeine/paracetamol tablets
A roll of sticking plaster
Imodium
Needle
Tweezers
Scissors
Crêpe bandage and safety pins
Two cling-wrap bandages

The contents of more elaborate medical kits will depend on the nature and duration of the excursion, and the level of medical expertise available in the party.

When a major safari-type expedition is undertaken, a doctor should be included in the party, and a comprehensive medical box or pack should be carried. This should include basic surgical instruments, fluids for intravenous administration, and a range of drugs and dressings.*

When all equipment must be carried in back-packs, medical supplies will, of necessity, be more limited. The doctor in the party is advised to carry two syringes and a number of needles, two ampoules of pentazocine or morphine, and ampoules of diazepam, adrenalin and an antihistamine. Small supplies of antispasmodic (hyoscine) anti-emetic (metoclopramide) and antacid *(Gelusil)* tablets should be included in the doctor's kit, along with 20 aspirin/codeine *(Codis)* or paracetamol/codeine *(Dolorol forte)* tablets and a five-day course of a broad spectrum antibiotic (amoxycillin). The carrying of snake bite antivenom is no longer recommended, as it is inactivated by long-term exposure to temperatures above 5°C *(see* Snake Bite).

When an extended excursion to a remote or inaccessible area is planned, and there is no doctor or trained nurse in the party, the matter of medical emergencies should be discussed, in advance, with the leader's usual doctor. He or she will be able to offer helpful advice and may be prepared to supply a syringe and one or two ampoules of strong pain-killer, with instructions for use in the event of serious injury.

* The doctor responsible for stocking the medical box may find it useful to consult the lists based on Everest and other expedition experiences which appear in papers published in the British Medical Journal: Nicol, H.G. 23 June 1979: pp. 1692–4; Illingworth, R. 17 January 1981: pp. 202–5.

LEADERSHIP AND MORALE

Every party on a hike, trail, climb or expedition should have a recognized leader: someone with considerable experience of outdoor life and good knowledge of the route to be followed. The leader should command the respect of the other members of the party and, in turn, will take responsibility for their well-being throughout the excursion. He or she will act in the best interests of every member of the party in the event of an emergency or accident.

A good leader should recognize the physical and mental resources of each member of the party and realize when these are being over-taxed. He or she should be able to exercise common sense in the face of unforeseen circumstances, and have the strength of purpose to take decisions which will serve the common good of the party. Other attributes are cheerfulness, a sense of humour, and genuine enjoyment of the company of others.

Field Marshal Montgomery defined leadership as the capacity and will to rally men and women to a common purpose. Leadership styles vary from rigidly autocratic to completely free-and-easy. Somewhere midway between these two extremes is probably the most effective in maintaining good morale in the party. Leadership skills of the sort necessary for successful expeditions are not inherently present – they are acquired in the course of experience over many years on hiking trails, climbing expeditions and similar outdoor excursions.

FINDING THE WAY

This is the responsibility of the leader. When there is a track or path to follow, it is good policy to stick to it. Sign posts obviously give useful information. It is common practice for mountaineers to build small cairns of stones at intervals along new or little used routes. These are easily recognized, and act as a guide for those following the route for the first time.

MAPS

A good map of the area and a compass are essential items of equipment, and map reading is a vital skill for the leader of any expedition. Maps have been drawn of most areas of South Africa and these represent the mapping gold standard (*see* page 138).

A scale of 1:50 000 is suitable for mountain traverses and cross-country hikes. Commercially produced maps of designated hiking trails and local areas (for example, Table Mountain) are also available. These vary in detail and accuracy, and care is necessary when selecting a map on which planning and subsequent route finding will be based.

MAP READING

By convention, the sidelines of a good quality map will approximate the direction of the North–South meridian. When reading in the field, it is advisable to orientate the map so that the top points to North (0°), and the bottom to South (180°). A rough indication of the position of North may be obtained in sunny weather by pointing the number 12 on a wristwatch in the direction of the sun. True North will lie midway between 12 and the position of the hour hand.

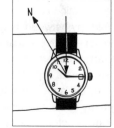

On a clear night, South is located by identifying the Southern Cross, a constellation of four bright stars, fairly low in the sky. Having identified the Southern Cross, look for two bright stars to the left-hand side. These are

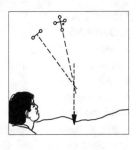

known as The Pointers. Draw an imaginary line extending down the long axis of the Southern Cross. Then draw a second line at right-angles to the mid-point of a line joining the two Pointers. Extend this line to cross the first line. South lies at the point of intersection (*see* illustration).

Prominent natural features, such as a hill top, mountain pass or survey beacon, which are visible from the map reader's position, can be identified once the map has been orientated. The directions of such features are referred to as bearings and these are expressed in degrees. A bearing of 90° is due East and a bearing of 270° is due West. The map reader's exact position on the map can be established as the point of intersection of the bearing lines.

USING A COMPASS

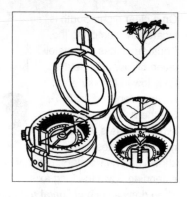

A bearing can be determined with a pocket compass by placing the instrument on a stable surface. The point of the compass needle will indicate North, and the bearing is the reading which corresponds to the direction of interest. A bearing is obtained with a prismatic compass by pointing the instrument in the desired direction and aligning the hair-line over a prominent natural feature. The bearing can then be read through the prism.

A compass in good working order will indicate Magnetic North. This is situated approximately 20° West of True North (1994). Allowance must be made for this magnetic variation when transferring compass bearings to a map and vice versa. To obtain map bearings, subtract 20° from compass readings; add 20° to map bearings to obtain the compass reading (*see* illustration below).

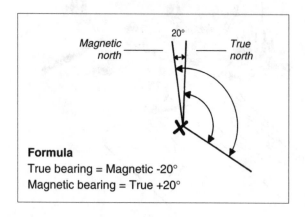

Formula
True bearing = Magnetic -20°
Magnetic bearing = True +20°

SETTING UP CAMP

Whenever nights in the open are planned, serious consideration should be given to carrying a light-weight tent. Several, sturdy, weatherproof models are available, and the protection and comfort they provide at night fully justify the extra weight (3–4 kg) carried by day. During winter, when rain and cold can be expected, it is irresponsible *not* to carry a tent on mountain traverses and overnight hikes.

If possible, the intended camping spot should be reached several hours before dark. The tent/s should be pitched on level ground, with the back to prevailing wind. Night-time comfort will be increased by removing stones and constructing a mattress of bracken (*slangbos*) under the groundsheet of the tent. Never pitch a tent in the dry bed of a stream or over an obvious

game path – serious sleep disturbance could be caused by a sudden rain storm or nocturnal foraging activity! If there is a stream near the camping place, water for drinking and cooking purposes should be obtained upstream, and dish washing and ablutions carried out downstream. 'Calls of nature' should be attended to at least fifty metres from both the tent and the source of water. If more than one night is going to be spent at a particular camping spot, a latrine pit should be dug in a suitably secluded spot and used by all members of the party. This will prevent widespread soiling of the area around the camping site. It is also advisable to dig a small rubbish pit. Both pits should be filled in when the party breaks camp.

FIREPLACES

Bush, forest and mountain fires devastate thousands of hectares of land every year during the dry seasons. For this reason, lighting cooking fires is prohibited in many mountain ranges, State forest lands and wilderness areas. Hikers and climbers in these proclaimed areas must carry small stoves for cooking purposes.

Where fires are permitted, extreme care must be taken to ensure that surrounding dry grass and brushwood does not catch light. An area sheltered from the wind should be cleared of foliage, and a fireplace constructed of large stones (the fire must

(a)

(b)

be confined within the limits of these stones (*see* illustration (a)). An alternative arrangement is a short trench 50 cm long, 20 cm deep, and narrow enough to support cooking pots (*see* illustration (b)).

Special attention must be given to the disposal of coals and ash when the fire is no longer required. Wood coals retain heat for a prolonged period of time, and may be fanned into flames by a breeze many hours after the fire is considered dead. Innumerable bush fires have been started in this way. If water is plentiful, some should be poured on the fireplace when the fire has burnt down. Unburnt wood fragments and ash should be stamped on and then covered with earth. The stones forming the perimeter of the fireplace can then be placed on top. A trench fireplace should be filled in with earth.

WATER
Life cannot be sustained without regular replacement of the water lost as urine, perspiration and on the breath. Without fluid intake, an individual will survive for no longer than four days. This interval is shorter under conditions of great heat or extreme exertion.

Daily water requirements vary according to activity level, diet, acclimatization and prevailing weather conditions. An average-sized adult with a semi-sedentary occupation will consume at least 1 500 ml of fluid in the course of a normal day's activities. This fact must be borne in mind when considering water requirements on a trail, hike or mountain climb with associated increased exertion and sweating.

Unless there is absolute assurance that water can be obtained along the route, each individual should carry a personal water-bottle with a capacity of 1 500 ml. This should be replenished whenever possible, preferably from a running water source such as a stream or spring. In hot conditions, and during strenuous exercise, an intake of 150–200 ml (one cupful) per hour should be maintained. The availability of water is clearly a major factor in determining the sites of overnight camps. In very dry conditions and in emergency situations it may be necessary to go to considerable lengths to obtain water. It is most likely to be found where vegetation is greenest, in natural hollows, and at the foot of hills. It is always worth sinking a long stick or reed into the sand of a dry river course. If, once withdrawn, the tip of the stick is moist, dig a hole up to 1,5 m deep in the riverbed. Water will seep into this from the surrounding sand and, in time, a useful quantity should collect. Small volumes of water may be collected as a result of condensation on the inside of a plastic bag placed over a leafy branch or a bunch of cut foliage. A solar still may be constructed if a large sheet of plastic (2 m x 2 m) is available. Increased temperature under the plastic sheet causes the air in the hole to become saturated with water vapour derived from the hot soil. This vapour condenses on the under-surface of the plastic and then runs into the container. A good solar

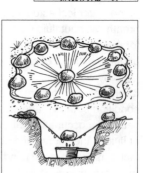

still will produce no more than 500 ml in 24 hours (*see also* Survival Kits). Water obtained from streams high in the mountains and in remote wilderness areas is usually pure and drinkable. Contamination must be assumed if there is dead animal matter in a water hole or stream, or if the source is close to or passes near human dwellings. The simplest way to make potentially infected water safe for drinking is to boil it. This involves fuel, but is necessary to avoid infection. Chlorination tablets and porous porcelain filters may be obtained commercially and should be considered when planning a major expedition.

Mountain Safety Guidelines

Mountains often turn out to be bigger than they seem on first inspection. Ravines conceal hazards like precipices and waterfalls; weather changes occur rapidly; paths are often poorly defined; and mist and darkness can obscure the route. Certain rules *must* be observed if mountain climbing is to be a pleasurable and accident-free recreation:

1 Never climb alone. Four is the ideal minimum so that in the event of an accident one can stay with the injured person and two can go for help.

2 Choose climbs within the ability and fitness of all members of the party.

3 Start out in good time so that the route up and down can be completed comfortably before dark.

4 The leader should have done both the route up and the route down before. Failing this he or she should carry a guide, map and compass, and know how to use them.

5 Before departure, make sure that someone at home knows the route to be followed and the expected time of return. This information is vital if the party is significantly overdue. Do not deviate from your planned route without very good reason.

6 The party should keep together and climb at a comfortable pace for the slowest member. It is dangerous to split up or take different paths.

7 Every member *must* carry a sweater, waterproof anorak and long trousers (tracksuit pants) no matter how mild the weather or how short the intended climb. These items, along with food, water-bottle and survival kit, should be carried in a backpack, leaving the hands free.

8 Before setting out, the leader should check that every member of the party has suitable footwear and is carrying the items listed under point 7.

9 Study the current weather forecast before setting out and watch weather developments. If gale-force winds, rain or extreme heat are imminent, it may be wise to postpone or cancel the climb. Turn back in good time if bad weather develops *en route*. It is wise to do this rather that to soldier on into a potential emergency situation.

10 If overtaken by darkness or thick mist and uncertain of the route, do not try to force your way down. This is inviting disaster. Find shelter out of the wind and stay put. If necessary, huddle together for warmth. When the mist lifts, or daylight returns, you will be intact and able to see the way.

11 If you lose your way or find yourself in an area which looks dangerous, go back the way you came. Do not push on into the unknown. If a path cannot be found, never descend an unknown ravine. There may be concealed rock-faces and waterfalls. Walk down broad slopes which permit clear vision of what lies ahead.

12 In the event of an accident, keep calm and prevent other members of the party from taking rash or hasty measures. Proceed in the manner outlined under *How to Handle an Accident*.

13 Ground parties may be difficult to spot from the air in the event of a helicopter search or rescue. Red, orange, yellow and silver are the colours most easily discerned from the air, and the task of the crew is made easier by laying out on the ground or waving brightly-coloured clothing or sleeping bags. By day, a reflector device may be used to attract attention. A confined smoky fire (green wood) is also effective, and permissible in an emergency situation.

With acknowledgements to the Mountain Club of South Africa.

IMPROVISING SHELTER

A properly pitched, good quality, lightweight tent provides ideal shelter in extreme weather conditions. In the absence of a tent, shelter must be improvised with whatever is available.

The cooling and debilitating effect of strong wind must never be underestimated. Simply getting out of the wind on the leeward side of a large rock, spur of hillside, or dense clump

of vegetation may make the difference between survival in good condition and severe hypothermia.

If a groundsheet and strong twine are carried, an effective two-person shelter can be constructed by placing the sheet over a simple frame of three sticks. The ends of the groundsheet are anchored to pegs driven into the ground. As a substitute for the stick frame, a short length of rope can be tied tightly between two trees. The walls of the shelter should be at an angle of 45° with

the ground to promote rain water drainage. Similar structures provide effective shelter from hot sunshine. If more that one groundsheet is available a larger shelter can be constructed.

Effective shelters can also be constructed from natural materials if these are available. A framework of sturdy sapling poles is erected. On either side, a lattice work of thinner sticks is established and then a thatch of reeds, bushes or long grass is tied into place. This type of shelter takes several hours to

build even when materials are readily to hand. Carefully constructed, it will provide good protection from the elements for several days.

LIGHTNING STRIKES

Every year, a number of people are killed by lightning strikes, while others suffer shock and serious burns. A lightning bolt is a surge of electrical energy with a strength of more than one-billion volts. Its path of descent has a diameter of five to seven metres. When the bolt strikes the earth, secondary flashes occur which may strike objects within a radius of thirty metres. A direct strike usually causes instant death. There may be a short period of ineffective contraction (fibrillation) before the heart stops beating. Near-miss victims suffer burns, lung damage from air concussion and tissue damage – particularly of the nervous system.

During an electrical storm it is *not* advisable to seek shelter under a tall, isolated tree, or in a hut or tent which is the only structure in a large, flat, open space. Lightning is drawn to the highest points in the storm area, so these are best avoided. Move down well below the summit of a mountain or crown of a hill, and shelter under low, evergreen trees or bushes. Good protection is provided by a rock over-hang or cave, if this is available. It is advisable to remain under cover until the storm has passed.

A victim of lightning strike who is not breathing must be subjected at once to cardio-respiratory resuscitation. If no neck pulse can be felt, deliver two or three forceful blows over the breast bone – this will sometimes restore the heartbeat. If there is no response, start external heart massage and continue until spontaneous heartbeat returns, or you are certain that the victim is dead. Less seriously injured individuals will require treatment for shock, pain and burns. Evacuation to hospital is advisable in every case as there may be internal injuries which are not immediately evident (*see* Artificial Respiration *and* Heart Attack).

FIRE

Mountain, forest and bush fires destroy many thousands of hectares of vegetation every year. These fires are occasionally started by lightning strikes or sparks generated by a large rolling boulder. Fires started deliberately by farmers to improve their grazing may sometimes get out of control. By far the most common causes of veld and forest fires are ill-tended cooking fires and carelessly discarded matches and cigarette ends.

In addition to the damage done to vegetation, a fire can claim the lives of any who become trapped in its path. It is vital, therefore, to know something about the development of bush and mountain fires, and how to avoid injury and death.

Fires are encouraged by dry vegetation, hot weather conditions, low relative humidity and wind. They are, therefore, more common during the dry season. A bush fire advances on a front driven by the wind. The burning front is seldom more than a few metres wide. Behind it is left a wasteland of ash and destroyed vegetation. A fire will always burn uphill rather than down. Narrow kloofs and ravines create a chimney-like effect and fire will race up these faster than a person can run. Heat and wind-blown flaming vegetation can cause outbreaks ahead of the main front. Individuals and animals in the line of advancement may thus find themselves trapped between two fires. When in the vicinity of a bush fire, observe the following guidelines:

1 Respect the ferocity of bush and mountain fires, and the speed at which flames can advance. Unless the fire is small and the wind gentle do not attempt to fight it. Effective fire-fighting requires special expertise and equipment, and is best left to those with the necessary training. Rather ensure your own safety and that of the party by moving well away from the burning area, preferably to a road or good escape path.

2 Remember that fires burn uphill. Never attempt to escape a mountain or hill fire by climbing in front of it. Move to one or other side of the line of advancement and work your way to windward, that is, in the opposite direction to the path of the fire. Keep to open slopes. Never go into a kloof or ravine where you could be trapped by dense vegetation, rock-faces, and fire racing up from below.

3 If close contact with the fire is unavoidable, cover yourself with clothing. A woollen balaclava, hat, long-sleeved jacket, gloves and long trousers will, to some extent, protect you from radiant heat and burns. A towel over the head and neck will help, as will a handkerchief held over the mouth and nose.

4 If trapped, *do not panic:* your survival depends on rational action. Look out for a break in the fire line; this may be where there is a clearing in the bush, a scree of loose stones, a large slab of surface rock, or a pathway. Use this as an escape route to the area which the fire has already burnt. If there is no obvious break, look for the place where the flames are at their lowest. Protect your face with green grass or bush if this is available. Take three deep breaths and hold the fourth in, keep your head low and run as quickly as you can until you are through the flames. Be prepared for great heat, and don't inhale until you are clear of the fire line. If you should stumble or fall, attempt to roll back on to your feet rather than putting your hands on burning vegetation. If your clothes are alight when you reach the burnt-out area, throw yourself to the ground and roll over and over. Throw loose earth on smouldering garments. Treat a companion whose clothes are on fire in the same way. Burns should then be treated, if feasible, by immersion in cold water as soon as possible. Paracetamol or codeine tablets will provide some pain relief. Subsequent management will depend on the extent and severity of the burns.

5 If an escape through the line of fire is out of the question, one of several other strategies may be employed. If there is time, a protective area should be cleared or burnt in the bush. Obviously, the larger the area the better. Those trapped should lie on the ground in the centre of this area with their heads covered until the fire line has passed beyond the clearing and they can make their escape to a burnt-out area. Another technique, when there are a number of individuals trapped, is for all to obtain fire-beating implements such as branches and form a circle facing outwards. With vigorous beating fire may be kept at bay round the perimeter of the circle until the fire line has passed. Survivors can then make their escape into the burnt-out area.

6 Fire consumes oxygen and produces very hot smoke. This can damage the upper airway, with potentially fatal consequences. The best air for breathing in a bush fire situation can be found close to the ground.

Anyone who is unable to move out of the path of heavy smoke clouds should lie on the ground and cover mouth and nose with a handkerchief or other piece of cloth.

RIVER CROSSING

Many rivers are shallow and can be crossed with ease at selected spots. However, heavy rain may rapidly change a gentle stream into a raging torrent, and a tranquil river into a major obstacle to progress. River crossing should always be approached with caution and an awareness of potential danger.

A flooded river may be avoided by taking an alternative route. If there is no other way round, it is prudent and sensible to camp next to a flooded river until the water level has dropped, rather than risk drowning or equipment loss. When coastal hikes and trails involve crossing estuaries, attention should be given to tide tables. A crossing which is extremely hazardous at high tide may be accomplished with ease by waiting for low tide. A dangerous river crossing may be justified *only* when the alternatives to crossing are more hazardous than the crossing itself, for example, overnight exposure to extreme weather conditions or unprotected climbing along a rock face. Under such circumstances the following precautions must be observed:

1 Select the site for crossing with care. Boulder-hopping may be feasible at certain places. Rapids indicate shallow rocky sections which may be easier to wade than even-flowing deeper reaches. Avoid crossing immediately above a waterfall where lost footing could have disastrous consequences.

2 Boulder-hopping ability varies from person to person and shorter members of the party may need a helping hand. Balance is improved by removing backpacks and passing them hand to hand. Beware of slippery rocks and logs.

3 When forced to wade, keep boots and socks on if the water is cold. This will prevent numbness, injury and stumbling. A stick will provide added support as will linking arms with other members of the party. If the current is swift, aim for a point on the opposite bank some way downstream. This will reduce the force of the current on your body.

4 A rope across the river is a highly desirable safe-guard whenever crossing appears hazardous. When swimming is the only option, the rope should be anchored firmly on the nearside and payed-out as the strongest swimmer in the party crosses the river with it tied around his or her waist. When the current is strong, it is advisable to select a far side anchor point some way downstream so that the rope crosses the river at an angle. A free-running clip and a sling can be used to link other members of the party to the safety rope once it has been anchored on both sides. Heavy backpacks compound the difficulty of a river crossing. If two ropes are available it may be possible to get them across the river using a cableway system.

Rescuing a Drowning Person

A non-swimmer may drown when he or she falls into a deep pool or gets out of depth during a river crossing. Good swimmers drown when swept away by strong currents or rendered unconscious in the water by a blow on the head. Almost all drowning deaths could have been prevented by exercising common sense. It is extremely rash to dive into a river or mountain pool without first checking its depth. No river crossing should be tackled without careful consideration of width, depth and strength of current (*see* River Crossing).

When someone in the water is clearly in difficulty, there should be no delay in providing assistance. It may be feasible to throw a rope or extend a tree branch for the person to grab, and so pull him- or herself to the side. If this is not possible, a swimmer should go to the rescue. A drowning person may panic and clutch a would-be rescuer so fiercely that swimming is impossible. The rescuer must be prepared to deal with this situation. If the victim is able

(a)

to respond to instructions, tell him or her to place his or her hands on the rescuer's shoulders from behind and to hold on (*see* illustration (a)). The rescuer will then have arms and legs free to swim breaststroke and can 'tow' the victim to safety. If the victim is unconscious, the rescuer must support his or her face above the water. A strong swimmer may be able to swim backwards with his hands on either side of the victim's head. It may prove easier to swim side-

(b)

stroke with one hand held under the victim's jaw or with an arm hooked under one of the victim's armpits (*see* illustration (b)).

In certain circumstances it may be advisable merely to support the victim above the water and to institute mouth-to-mouth resuscitation until further assistance arrives.

A would-be rescuer who is grabbed in a bear hug by a panic-stricken drowning person must release her- or himself before attempting further rescue. This is achieved by bringing a hand up between the victim's arms and pushing his or her head forcefully backwards (*see* illustration (c)). If this does not cause release, flex your hip and knee so that your lower leg is against the victim's chest and then push forcefully against his or her trunk until the grasp is released (*see* illustration (d)).

(c)

If an arm is grasped, release the grip by twisting the arm to exert firm pressure against the victim's thumb. Once the drowning person has been brought to the shore treatment is as outlined in the sections on Artificial Respiration, and Drowning.

(d)

USE OF A RADIO

Radio communication is used extensively by rescue services and the police. Search and rescue parties are able to keep in touch with the base using portable handsets.

A standard portable radio has an on/off switch which regulates volume, a channel indicator, a transmit button and a 'squelch' button. When the radio is switched on to the correct channel, messages will be received. To transmit, it is necessary to depress the transmit button. This should be released as soon as the sender has finished speaking so that the response can be heard.

Portable radios work well when there is 'line of sight', with no major natural features between sender and receiver. When mountains intervene, or one party is in a deep ravine, contact will be lost unless intervening 'repeater' stations have been established. Communication with aircraft is feasible provided the correct channels are used.

When using a portable radio, hold the speaker in front of your lips. Speak slightly more slowly than usual, but at normal conversation volume; it is not necessary to shout. Use short sentences and check at intervals that your message has been understood. Remember to release the transmit button when you are ready to receive.

Portable radios are battery-operated. When in continuous use, a battery should last in the region of four to six hours.

A to Z
OF OUTDOOR
FIRST AID
AND MEDICAL
EMERGENCIES

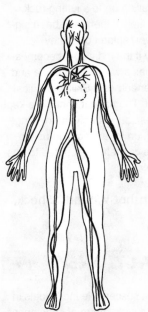

ABDOMINAL INJURIES

Abdominal injuries can be described as 'open' or 'closed'. In both cases there may be serious damage to internal organs. An *open* injury is present when the abdominal wall has been penetrated by a sharp object and a channel exists between the exterior and the abdominal cavity. Infection is a strong possibility. A *closed* injury may follow any serious blow to the abdomen, for example, falling on to a jutting rock. Internal haemorrhage is likely if there has been significant damage to the liver, spleen or kidney.

Suspect serious injury if the individual becomes pale, cold and clammy, has a weak rapid pulse and generalized abdominal tenderness. Skilled surgical management is essential. The patient should be kept warm and at complete rest, and not given anything to eat or drink. If feasible, an intravenous infusion should be set up, and the casualty evacuated to hospital as quickly as possible.

See also **Bleeding, Gunshot Wounds, Shock, Stab Wounds**

ALLERGIC REACTIONS

Allergic reactions occur in susceptible individuals in response to contact with a wide range of substances. Pollen, grass seeds, dusts, certain types of food, drugs and insect bites may all act as *allergens.* In sensitive subjects, allergens evoke a chemical response which may cause hay fever, a skin rash, an asthma attack, swelling of the body or even, in rare instances, total collapse (anaphylaxis). Individuals tend to respond in the same way whenever they are exposed to a particular allergen. Those sensitive to pollens and grasses develop hay fever and an indi-

44

vidual who reacts to shellfish is likely to develop a
rash and swelling whenever this type of seafood is
eaten. Most allergic reactions are relatively mild and
subside when contact with the allergen is avoided.

Relief may be obtained with an antihistamine drug
but this may cause associated drowsiness. There are
a number of effective prescription medicines for hay
fever. Respiratory obstruction due to vocal cord
swelling and anaphylactic collapse (*see* Bee Stings)
call for emergency treatment. Artificial ventilation
(*see* Artificial Respiration) of the lungs must be initiated if respiration is failing. Injections of adrenaline and
cortisone are urgently necessary to halt this acute
allergic process.

See also **Asthma, Shock**

AMPUTATION

Victims of shark and crocodile attacks may suffer
traumatic amputation of a limb or part thereof.
Complete severance of a limb may also occur in a
motor vehicle accident. Blood loss and shock in such
situations are life-threatening, and immediate steps
must be taken to counteract these. A large dressing,
towel or other clean cloth must be placed over the
wound and firmly compressed. This will usually
staunch bleeding, but if obvious arterial bleeding continues (indicated by bright red, spurting blood) a ligature (a piece of cord or bandage) should be tied
tightly above the wound and the stump elevated. The
ligature should never be left in place for more than
15–20 minutes at a time, and should be removed as
soon as the bleeding is under control. If feasible, an
intravenous infusion should be set up, and a strong
pain-killer administered. It is preferable to bring aid to
the casualty rather than transport him or her to skilled
care. Primary treatment should be given at the site of

the incident and the casualty moved only when blood loss has been replaced, the pulse rate has decreased and the pain-killer is working well. The amputated limb should accompany the casualty to hospital as surgical restoration is sometimes possible. The limb should be wrapped in a clean cloth.

See also **Bleeding, Shock**

ANIMAL BITES

Two aspects must be considered in the case of an animal bite – the wound and possible infection. Wounds vary from a few small skin punctures to extensive lacerations with blood loss and underlying bone fracture. Most animals carry a multitude of organisms in their mouths which cause serious infection when implanted in human tissues. Rabies is endemic in certain small wild animal species in South Africa and is transmitted by bites. The first consideration when treating an animal bite should be thorough cleansing of the wound. After applying pressure to arrest bleeding, the wound should be bathed for a prolonged period in running water. If this is not possible, clean water from a water-bottle should be used. A clean, dry dressing can then be applied and the casualty made comfortable. If an antibiotic is available, this should be administered. Extensive injury with much blood loss may be accompanied by shock and collapse. If this occurs, an intravenous drip should be set up and the victim transferred to hospital as soon as possible. Bearing in mind the likelihood of infection, it is advisable to consult a doctor about any significant animal bite. A booster injection of antitetanus serum is often indicated and a course of anti-rabies injections may be advisable.

See also **Rabies, Shock**

Ankle injuries

Ankle injury occurs when a sudden sharp twisting force is applied to the joint, for example by slipping on loose gravel or wet grass. Damage may be done to the ligaments which surround the ankle, to the bones which make up the joint or to both. Blood or fluid may collect in the cavity of the joint, and pain is usually immediate. Swelling follows rapidly, and any movement of the joint is likely to cause discomfort. If the ligaments round the ankle have merely been stretched (sprained), recovery will occur spontaneously with rest over a number

of days. If, however, ligaments have been torn, bleeding has occurred into the joint or there is bony injury, skilled medical treatment is necessary. In the period immediately after injury, swelling and tenderness may make assessment of the injury very difficult. At this stage it is often impossible to determine by simple examination whether the lower ends of the two leg bones (tibia and fibula) remain intact. X-ray examination is therefore necessary in most cases. While awaiting further treatment the injured joint should be bandaged lightly but firmly with a crêpe bandage, and elevated on a cushion or some other support (*see* illustration). Codeine or paracetamol tablets will relieve pain.

See also Fractures, Sprains and Strains

APPENDICITIS

The appendix is a thin, blind-ended tube found in the lower abdominal cavity on the right-hand side. It is 4–9 cm long and it opens into the large intestine close to the junction with the small intestine. It has no known function in human beings. Acute inflammation

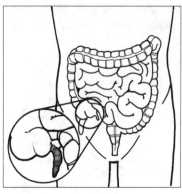

in the appendix (*see* illustration) may arise spontaneously, or follow obstruction to its opening into the large intestine. Initially, an individual with appendicitis feels unwell, may vomit and pass loose stools. He/she develops generalized abdominal discomfort and pain centred around the umbilicus (navel). After several hours the pain shifts to the right lower quadrant of the abdomen and the person will be extremely tender to touch in this area. Any movement increases discomfort. Body temperature is usually raised.

If the appendix bursts, infection may spread to the tissues surrounding the intestines and lining the abdominal wall (peritonitis). A patient with acute appendicitis requires surgical treatment, and should be evacuated to a hospital as soon as possible. If this can be accomplished in 2–4 hours, the patient should not be given food or fluids by mouth. If many hours are likely to elapse before a hospital is reached, small quantities of water (50–100 ml) may be drunk at intervals to maintain hydration. An antibiotic should be administered if available.

ARTIFICIAL RESPIRATION

Permanent tissue damage is likely if the human brain is deprived of oxygen for more than two minutes and death will occur after five or six minutes. When breathing stops for any reason it becomes a matter of great urgency to ventilate the lungs artificially until normal respiration has been re-established. Artificial respiration is most efficiently achieved by mouth-to-mouth breathing:

1 Lay the casualty on his or her back.

2 Inspect the mouth cavity and, if necessary, use your fingers to remove dentures, foodstuffs or foreign matter which could cause obstruction.

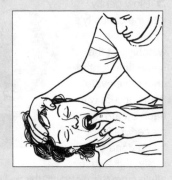

3 Elevate the chin so that the neck is extended.

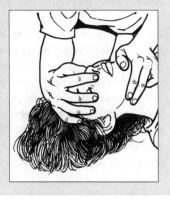

4 Place your lips over the casualty's lips, using the fingers of one hand to secure an airtight seal. Pinch the nostrils shut with the fingers of the other hand.

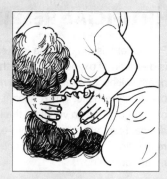

5 Blow gently into the casualty's mouth while watching at the same time for the chest to elevate. If this occurs with each breath, the procedure is being done correctly. If the casu-

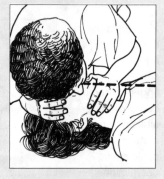

alty's stomach distends, this indicates that the chin has not been elevated sufficiently.

About 16 breaths are required each minute. If there is associated heart arrest, external cardiac compression must be co-ordinated with artificial respiration. This is best done by two people working together. The individual providing cardiac massage should pause after every fouth compression to allow inflation of the chest. When only one rescuer is present, he or she should compress the chest 10 times between each inflation.

6 If the victim is a small child, efficient ventilation is best achieved by placing the lips over the nose and the mouth.

See also **Heart Attack, Shock**

ASPHYXIATION

Asphyxiation occurs when the flow of oxygen into the lungs is interrupted. It may be due to a marked decrease in the oxygen content of the air being breathed or result from an obstruction to the nose and mouth, or the air passages leading to the lungs. Situations inducing asphyxia include sitting round a coal or coke brazier in a poorly ventilated space, being trapped in a collapsed underground tunnel, smothering under soft fabrics (particularly children), drowning, and inhaling foodstuffs or a foreign body. A person is likely to die within a few minutes if access to fresh air is not rapidly restored.

If the asphyxiated individual is not breathing, artificial respiration must be instituted without delay and continued until spontaneous breathing returns. If there is no heartbeat, external cardiac compression must be co-ordinated with mouth-to-mouth respiration and continued until the neck pulse (carotid) returns or the individual is pronounced dead.

See also **Artificial Respiration, Choking, Heart Attack**

ASTHMA

Asthma is a common condition, particularly in children. The symptoms are due to a generalized narrowing of the smallest air passages in the lungs. This is brought on in susceptible subjects by inhaling certain pollens, dusts or fumes, or eating certain foodstuffs. Asthma attacks can also be induced by infection, physical exertion and emotional disturbance. During an attack, breathing is rapid and laboured, with marked difficulty and prolongation in the breathing out phase. The chest remains expanded and a wheeze is clearly audible. The subject becomes distressed and exhausted.

Most asthma patients are able to limit and control their symptoms with pump inhalers and prescribed medication. During any expedition or camping holiday these should be used regularly as prescribed. Situations which are known to bring on an attack, such as over-exertion, should be avoided. It may be unwise to undertake a long country trail during the pollen season.

Before the start of a hike or expedition, the leader should be told if a member of the party is prone to asthma attacks.

Should an asthma attack occur, the individual should be made to rest; a semi-sitting position may be more comfortable than lying down. If a pump inhaler is being carried, two puffs should be administered. This can be repeated after half an hour if the response has been poor. The individual should be reassured and encouraged to drink small amounts of water. If there is no improvement after an hour, steps should be taken to obtain medical care. Severe asthma is potentially life-threatening and hospital treatment is often necessary.

See also **Allergic Reactions**

BACK AND NECK INJURIES

The individual bones of the spine are called vertebrae. Each vertebra consists of a body and a vertebral arch. The vertebral arches form a continuous passage called the spinal canal (*see* illustration). This runs behind the vertebral bodies and carries the spinal cord which connects the brain to the chest, abdomen and limbs. If vertebrae are fractured, crushed or displaced, the spinal cord may be distorted, lacerated or even sev-

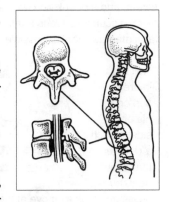

ered. Such damage will cause immediate paralysis and loss of feeling below the injury. Neck and back injuries occur as a result of direct blows, sudden distorting forces, penetrating wounds and falls from heights. It is often impossible to determine the extent of an injury until X-rays have been taken. An individual with a neck or back injury must be handled with great care as spinal cord damage can be caused or aggravated by uncontrolled movement.

The neck should be splinted by wrapping a towel, jersey or other thick garment round it. The detachable padded belt of a backpack may also be used. Splinting must be achieved with minimum of movement of the head, and

the casualty with a neck or back injury must be kept at complete rest on a firm surface, and conveyed only on a wooden backboard or other rigid support.

Ideally, the casualty should not be moved at all if medical assistance is close at hand. When movement is essential, the technique of 'log rolling' should be used. Spinal injury may cause a marked drop in blood pressure and slowing of the pulse (neurogenic shock). If feasible, an intravenous infusion should be set up, and a pain-killing drug administered if there is much discomfort. Transport to hospital should be facilitated as soon as possible.

Roll the injured person on to his or her side in such a manner that shoulders, trunk,  pelvis and legs all move at the same time.

Position the backboard against the casualty's back.

Log roll the casualty back into a supine position.

See also **Shock, Slipped Disc**

BEE STINGS

In the normal course of events, bees only sting if directly threatened or harassed. At certain times of the year, however, wild bees may become aggressive and attack without provocation. Escape from an angry swarm is best achieved by running through bushes; some protection is afforded by covering your head with a jacket or other garment.

An isolated sting causes sharp pain. Within minutes, redness and local swelling will be evident at the site of the sting and this may extend to the surrounding skin. There may be intense itching and, in loose tissue such as the eyelid, swelling may be impressive. Redness and swelling will subside in a matter of hours. Isolated stings are serious only in those instances when a bee has entered the mouth and swelling occurs in the throat or at the entrance to the windpipe (*see* Choking *for treatment*). Certain individuals are allergic to bee venom and a single sting may trigger an anaphylactic reaction (*see* Allergic Reactions). In these cases, there is rapid development of a generalized skin rash, massive swelling of the face and throat, breathing difficulty and collapse. Coma and death follow swiftly if the reaction is not reversed. A response of this nature usually follows previous bee stings, and reactions of increasing severity warn of possible anaphylaxis.

It is inadvisable to remove bee stings with tweezers, as compression of the sac may inject more venom. The sting should be removed by scraping a knife blade sideways across the skin. Local relief may be obtained by applying an

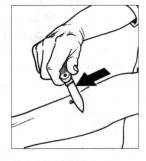

ice pack (if this is available) or antihistamine cream. An anaphylactic reaction calls for a prompt injection of adrenalin. Hypersensitive individuals should always carry an ampoule or two of adrenaline and a syringe when there is the likelihood of encountering bees.

See also **Allergic Reactions**

BILHARZIA

This infection is also known as schistosomiasis. Adult schistosoma worms live in large veins in the abdominal cavity. Eggs from the worms erode into the bladder and rectum, and are passed in urine and stools. On reaching a river or dam, these eggs release microscopic forms called miracidia which invade the bodies of certain strains of snail. In time, further microscopic forms called cerceria are released from the snails into the water. These are capable of burrowing through unbroken human skin and invading the bloodstream. Bilharzia is acquired by paddling or swimming in waterways inhabited by infested snails. Invasion may be recognized by a feeling of skin irritation shortly after leaving the water. This has been called 'swimmer's itch'. The most characteristic symptom of bilharzia is the passage of blood in the urine, particularly in the last few drops voided. Microscopic examination of the urine will reveal the presence of schistosoma eggs. When rectal infection is present blood is passed with the stools. Untreated, bilharzia may cause chronic bladder scarring, with a predisposition to recurrent infections and cancer. An effective drug is available to treat the condition.

Bilharzia occurs mainly in the Transvaal, Natal and the Eastern Cape. It is unwise to paddle or swim in rivers and dams in these areas.

BLEEDING

Blood is pumped by the heart, under pressure, through the arterial system. This blood is rich in oxygen and appears bright red. The smallest arteries end in a system of very fine, thin-walled vessels called capillaries. These supply body tissues with oxygen, glucose and other essential substances. The capillary network then joins up to form larger vessels called veins. These carry blood from the tissues back to the heart and lungs. Venous blood is under low pressure and is dark red.

External bleeding originates from wounds which are easily identified. When an artery has been punctured, the blood is bright red and spurts in time with the heart beat. Venous blood wells up and out of a wound at a slower rate. Capillary bleeding is seldom more than an ooze. All forms of bleeding will stop in response to sustained direct pressure. A large dressing, a towel or other piece of clean cloth should be placed on the wound and pressed firmly against the bleeding area (*see* illustration overleaf). Pressure must be maintained until it is clear that bleeding has stopped. If the wound is extensive, it may be advis-

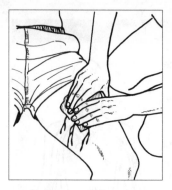

able to leave the compression dressing in place and bandage over it. Tourniquets (ligatures around limbs) are potentially very dangerous and should be used only when major vessels have been severed, for example, in traumatic amputation. No tourniquet should ever be left in place for longer than 15–20 minutes as blood flow to the limb is completely obstructed and there is very real danger of permanent tissue damage and the development of gangrene.

Internal bleeding occurs when there are serious fractures, or organs such as the liver, spleen or kidneys have been damaged. Loss of blood is not visible. The casualty will appear pale and feels cold and clammy, and the pulse becomes rapid and weak. These signs indicate shock, and hospital management is urgently needed. While waiting to be moved, the casualty should be kept at rest with the legs raised above the level of the rest of the body. If feasible, an intravenous infusion should be set up and a pain-killing injection administered. He or she should be covered with jackets or a sleeping bag, but not overwarmed. Small sips of water may be given if thirst is severe.

See also **Face and Nose Injuries, Shock**

BLINDNESS

Vision may be lost or seriously impaired if there is damage to any one of the four important structures in the eye. The highly sensitive, transparent *cornea* allows light to enter the eyeball. It also protects the interior of the eye from infection. The blue, green or brown *iris* controls the amount of light which passes to the back of the eye. It causes the pupil to dilate in dark surroundings and constrict in response to bright light. Behind the iris lies the *lens.* This alters shape, as necessary, to ensure that distant and nearby objects can be clearly focused on the *retina.* The retina is made up of layers of specialized nerve cells which convert light energy into electrical energy. This energy is transported along nerve pathways to an area of the brain where the signals are 'read' as visual images.

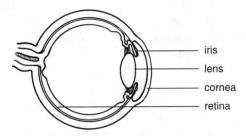

- iris
- lens
- cornea
- retina

Blindness may be a consequence of any serious eye injury (*see* Eye Injuries). It may also occur after severe head injury if there has been damage to areas of the brain which translate visual signals into recognized images (cortical blindness).

Temporary blindness may result from inflammation of the cornea, which is usually brought on by excessive exposure to the sun's ultraviolet rays. This is most likely to occur at high altitudes, in desert conditions (sun blindness) and on snowfields (snow blindness). The disabling condition develops hours after exposure and starts as a feeling of intense eye irritation. This is followed by profuse watering, swelling of the eyelids and difficulty in opening the eyes. It can be avoided by wearing good quality sunglasses or goggles when travelling in conditions of bright sunlight. Established cases take several days to recover. Acute pain can be relieved with anaesthetic eye drops, and should be followed with antibiotic eyes drops and bandaging the eyes. Pain relief can be achieved with codeine or paracetamol. The victim should be discouraged from rubbing the eyes.

See also Eye Injuries

Blisters

Attention to the feet is an important aspect of self care during any hike or walking tour. To avoid blisters, socks should be thick and boots should be well worn-in and comfortable. It is advisable to stop at the first sensation of friction so that footwear can be adjusted and chafed areas of skin covered with plasters before blistering occurs. Once a blister has formed it should be left intact. Cover liberally with several layers of plaster as this reduces the chance of infection. The blister will reabsorb over several days. Very large blisters may have to be pricked using a sterile needle. Prick a few tiny holes round the base of the blister to release fluid and then cover with mercurochrome and layers of plaster. At the end of the day, the feet should be washed and the plasters renewed.

Boils

A boil occurs when a hair follicle or oil gland in the skin becomes infected with bacteria called staphylococci. A red swelling develops under the skin and enlarges rapidly. It is extremely sensitive to touch and causes throbbing pain which is aggravated by movement. Body temperature may become elevated. After several days, the centre of the boil liquefies and then discharges onto the skin. This is usually associated with considerable relief of symptoms and healing. It is traditional to treat boils with warm poultices in an attempt to hasten discharge. Lancing should be attempted only when the presence of pus is obvious and the skin over the boil has thinned. A discharging boil should be covered with a dry dressing and renewed regularly. Recurrent boils suggest colonization of the nose with staphylococci. This should be treated with an antibiotic nasal cream.

Bruises

A bruise is due to bleeding below an intact skin surface. This bleeding may be in the deeper layers of the skin, the subcutaneous tissues or in muscle. As red cells and other blood components break down, the bruise changes colour from purple to dark blue to green, yellow and then a fading brown. Most bruises heal spontaneously, and rest and pain relief are all that is necessary. Finger-tip bruises can cause intense throbbing pain if there is blood in the confined space under a nail. Relief is obtained by boring a small hole in the centre of the nail with the tip of a clean,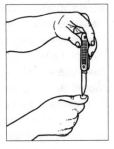

61

sharp knife, thus easing the pressure. Large bruises
may become infected and require surgical drainage.
Medical assistance is indicated if bruising is extensive, the individual becomes feverish or there is the
possibility of underlying fractures.

See also **Fractures**

BURNS AND SCALDS

Burns are caused by fire and by direct contact with
very hot objects and certain chemicals. Scalds are
caused by hot liquids. The injury is essentially the
same and is traditionally described as first, second or
third degree, depending on the depth and extent of
tissue damage. A more practical classification is
'superficial' and 'deep'. Superficial burns heal easily
with little permanent scarring. Deep burns are associated with shock and infection. Scars and deformity
are a common outcome and hospital management
is essential.

The burnt area should be immersed in cold water
as soon as possible and kept there for at least 15
minutes. This applies equally to fire burns, scalds
and burns caused by chemicals. If immersion is not
feasible, the burn should be covered with cloths
wrung-out in cold water. Do not apply any ointments
or creams and do not break blisters or attempt to
remove charred tissue. When pain is relieved the
wound should be covered with several layers of
dressings and lightly bandaged. Shock is almost
inevitable if superficial burns extend over more than
10% of the body's surface or there is damage to
deep tissues. If feasible, an intravenous infusion
should be set up and an antibiotic administered.
Pain-killers should be taken at regular intervals, and
urgent transfer to hospital must be arranged.
Burns usually result from negligence and will not

occur if proper care is taken with stoves, lamps, candles and cooking fires. Cans of petrol and other flammable fluids should be labelled clearly and kept well away from naked flame. If clothing catches fire, a blanket, coat or other heavy cloth should be used to smother the flames. The same effect can be achieved by rolling the individual on the ground or dousing the burning garment with water.

See also Shock

CHEST INJURIES

Chest injuries, like abdominal injuries, may be 'open' or 'closed'. Open injuries are caused by bullets and sharp objects which penetrate the chest wall and damage the heart, lungs and major blood vessels. Bullet and knife wounds are usually fatal if the heart or a major blood vessel has been pierced. If a lung has been pierced, air may issue from the entry wound with each breath. The dangerous condition of tension pneumothorax may arise if air is sucked into the pleural cavity with each breath and not expelled. This leads to increasing distension on one side of the chest, and compression of the underlying lung, with increasing respiratory difficulty. This is life threatening and calls for immediate decompression of the pleural cavity. Insert the largest bore needle available into a rib space at the side of the chest (*see* illustration overleaf). Push it in until a flow of air under pressure indicates that the pneumothorax has been entered. This should bring about immediate improvement in the patient's well-being. Breathing will become easier and less rapid. Secure the needle in place, manually if necessary, until formal chest drainage is possible. If a large needle is not available, the same effect may be achieved with the barrel of a pen after the ink cartridge has been removed. It will be necessary to make a small incision in the skin with a knife before inserting the pen barrel.

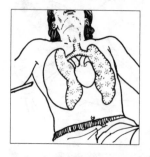 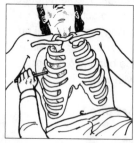

An individual with an open chest injury should be kept at rest, with the legs elevated slightly above the level of the trunk. The entry (and exit) wound should be covered with a dry dressing (*see* illustration below). An intravenous infusion should be set up if feasible.

Closed chest injuries most often occur as a result of motor vehicle accidents and falls. Rib fractures cause intense local tenderness and pain which is aggravated by respiration. Multiple rib fractures may interfere with the bellows mechanism of the chest to the extent that artificial ventilation becomes necessary.

Rib fractures are splinted with adhesive strapping over the damaged area. The strapping must be applied tightly and should extend beyond the midline of the chest both in front and behind (*see* illustration). An X-ray examination is required to determine the extent of a closed chest injury. The casualty should be kept at rest, treated for shock and transported to hospital as soon as possible.

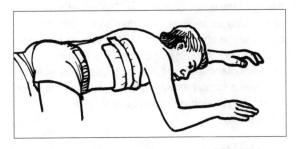

See also **Abdominal Injuries, Gunshot Wounds, Shock, Stab Wounds**

CHEST PAIN

Chest pain is a feature of a wide variety of conditions, and associated symptoms may help to identify the cause. Pain in muscles over the front of the chest and back may follow unusual exertion, particularly if this involves much lifting and pulling. Continuing with these activities increases the pain, and the muscles are tender to touch. Very severe muscle pain occurs in a condition called Bornholm's disease or 'devil's grip'. The pain is usually unilateral and aggravated by respiratory movement. It is caused by a viral infection and, consequently, several members of a group may be affected at the same time. Pain may last for three to seven days. Relief is obtained with codeine or paracetamol. Severe unilateral chest pains may precede an attack of shingles (Herpes zoster infection). Subsequent skin inflammation and blistering in a band round the chest make the diagnosis clear. Pleurisy is inflammation of the membranes which cover the surface of the lung and the inner wall of the chest cavity. This inflammation may occur in isolation, but more frequently occurs in association with an underlying pneumonia. The individual affected will become feverish, with shallow rapid breathing and flaring of the wings of the nose. The site of the pain can usually be indicated. Cardiac pain is felt in the centre of the chest. There may be radiation up to the neck and down the inside of the left arm. It may arise spontaneously or follow effort, such as walking up a steep slope (angina). It has a crushing constricting quality; the individual will be distressed, pale and clammy.

See also **Heart Attack, Pneumonia**

Childbirth

This is a natural process and, in the majority of cases, is accomplished without complications.
It should ideally take place in a hospital or at home, with skilled supervision and ready access to the facilities necessary for managing complications.
It is, therefore, inadvisable for women to join expeditions or travel to remote areas during the last months of pregnancy.

The onset of labour is usually heralded by backache and some vaginal discharge. This is followed by recurrent episodes of back and abdominal discomfort during which the womb contracts and hardens.
This process, the first stage of labour, lasts from two hours to twelve or more. This results in the gradual opening of the mouth of the womb. When the mouth of the womb is fully open, expulsion of the baby is possible. This is referred to as the second stage of labour. Contractions increase in frequency and strength, and the mother assists the passage of the baby's head down her vagina by straining with her

abdominal muscles. Once the head has been delivered, the rest of the infant's body follows rapidly.
A woman in labour should never be left on her own.
During contractions in the first stage she should be
encouraged to relax all her muscles until the pain
passes. Gentle massage over the small of the back
may aid relaxation. In the second stage she should
be encouraged to push down as hard as she can
during each contraction. As soon as the baby has
been delivered, the mouth and nose should be wiped
clean. If respiration does not start spontaneously in
the first minute, it may be necessary to blow gently
into the mouth and nose to effect ventilation. Once
good breathing has been established the umbilical
cord can be tied firmly with clean string or tape and
cut. The newborn infant should be wrapped in a
towel or cloth and given to the mother to hold. The
mother's womb will expel the afterbirth spontaneously, and thereafter blood loss is usually only slight.
No traction should be applied to the cord. If severe
bleeding occurs the womb should be massaged gently through the lower abdominal wall. This will promote natural contraction, the expulsion of clots and
the cessation of haemorrhage.

See also **Artificial Respiration, Bleeding**

Choking

Choking occurs when the voice box (larynx) or the
windpipe (trachea) are obstructed. The obstruction
may be due to inhaled food or some other foreign
body, or be caused by external compression of the
neck as in accidental or deliberate hanging. Partial
obstruction causes a bout of severe coughing. When
obstruction is complete, breathing ceases and the
individual's face turns blue. Death occurs within a
few minutes if the obstruction is not relieved.

A child who has inhaled food or a foreign body should be suspended head down by the legs and slapped between the shoulder blades. This will often dislodge an object obstructing the throat or larynx.

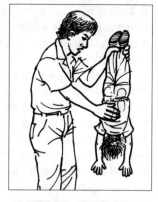

An older individual who has inhaled food may be subjected to the Heimlech manoeuvre, which entails grasping the person from behind, around the stomach, and applying a very forceful 'hug' (see illustration).

The upward movement of the diaphragm and forced expiration induced will often eject the obstructing object from the upper respiratory passage. Repeat the manoeuvre several times. If total obstruction persists, it becomes a matter of great urgency to get fresh air into the individual's lungs. This can be achieved using a large bore injection needle in the manner illustrated on the following page.

If a needle is not available, a small incision should be made with a sharp knife through the skin at the lower end of the Adam's apple and then through the membrane of the windpipe. It will be necessary to keep the tissues apart to allow passage of air.

See also **Asphyxiation**

1 Locate the angled anterior edge of the person's Adam's apple with your finger.

2 Trace this edge downwards in the direction of the chest. Immediately beyond the end of the Adam's apple there is a small depression or hollow.

3 Push the needle firmly into this hollow until air flows out. Sufficient air can pass through the needle to sustain life, but it will have to be held in position until expert help arrives.

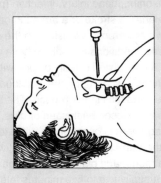

CONCUSSION

Concussion is induced by a severe blow to the head. It is a transitory state of abnormal brain function during which the victim shows impaired consciousness and loss of usual behaviour patterns. Concussion is not necessarily associated with skull fracture, intracranial bleeding or brain damage. Full recovery is usual although amnesia may persist for events immediately prior to the injury and during the period of concussion. An individual who has sustained concussion requires careful observation until there is a return to normal function. Decreasing responsiveness and a slow pulse rate indicate a rise in intracranial pressure and the need for urgent transfer to hospital.

See also **Head Injuries, Unconsciousness**

CONVULSIONS

A convulsion or seizure is the outward manifestation of sudden, excessive, uncontrolled electrical discharge from the surface layers of the brain. This discharge may be triggered by a lack of oxygen, poisoning, head injury, infection (meningitis, cerebral malaria), a stroke or a brain tumour. Individuals who have *recurrent* convulsions in the absence of any of these conditions are said to have epilepsy.

A convulsion usually begins with dramatic suddenness, whereupon the individual loses consciousness and falls to the ground. The body stiffens and the face becomes flushed or blue. After 30 seconds or so, there is onset of repetitive jerking movements in the trunk and arms. Frothy saliva may come from the mouth and bladder control may be lost. Eventually, usually two to five minutes later, jerking ceases and the individual passes into a relaxed state. This may be followed by a return to full consciousness or a period of natural sleep. Most convulsions will terminate spontaneously.

The person's head should be supported in a position which will promote unobstructed breathing. This is most easily achieved by lifting the chin until the neck is slightly extended. This will ensure an open airway through the nose and throat. It is not necessary (and is indeed dangerous) to insert something between the teeth. Tongue biting is not prevented by such a measure and teeth may be dislodged. It is physically

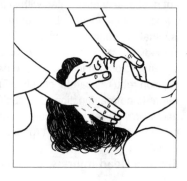

70

impossible to 'swallow' the tongue. An individual should be protected from self-injury during a seizure, for example, kicking against sharp objects, fire etc.

See also **Epilepsy**

CRAMP

Cramps are involuntary sustained strong contractions (spasms) of muscles. They can cause acute pain and tend to occur after unusual exertion, particularly if there has been salt loss from excessive sweating or diarrhoea. Cramp usually starts suddenly after a strong movement. The affected muscle is hard and tender. Relief is achieved by stretching the muscle to its limit.

Cramp in the calf is treated by pushing hard on the sole of the foot so that the toes point towards the shin. Cramp in the front of the thigh is treated by straightening the knee. Massaging the affected muscle will also aid pain relief. The affected individual should drink plenty of water and eat some salty food if cramps have been preceded by salt and water loss.

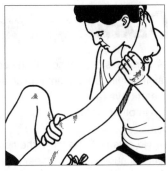

Cuts

The seriousness of a cut depends upon its depth and position. Cuts which go no deeper than the layers of the skin will soon heal. Deep cuts, however, may involve arteries and tendons with haemorrhage and loss of muscle function.

Muscle tendons run close to the surface of the skin on hands and feet, and round major joints such as the wrist and ankle. Thus deep cuts in these regions may have more serious consequences than cuts on the thigh or forearm.

Bleeding from a cut can always be controlled by direct pressure. The two sides of a small superficial cut can be joined with strips of plaster, whereas more extensive cuts may require stitching.

To minimize the chance of infection, the wound should be cleaned with an antiseptic solution and covered with gauze and a bandage or plaster. When there is a deep cut on the hand, foot, or close to a joint, movements should be tested.

The loss of ability to flex and extend any joint below the level of a deep cut suggests tendon damage. Skilled surgery is then necessary to restore function.

See also **Bleeding**

Death

A person is dead when all the accepted physical signs of life are absent and all attempts to restart the heart have failed.

In other words:

■ No pulse can be felt in the neck and no heart beat is audible when an ear is placed on the chest.

■ There is no respiratory movement of the chest and no condensation forms on a mirror or metal surface held in front of the nose and mouth.
■ The pupils are widely dilated and show no response at all to bright torch light.
■ There is no response at all to painful stimuli such as pinching.

External cardiac massage and artificial ventilation should be continued if there is any uncertainty about the signs of death. This applies particularly if the body is very cold, for example, after prolonged immersion or exposure in freezing weather conditions. Revival in such instances has occurred after rewarming and indicates that attempts at resuscitation should be continued until body temperature has been raised to the normal range.

Efforts to retrieve the body of a dead person should not be made if these would in any way cause danger to other members of the party. When death occurs in remote mountain or jungle areas, removal of the body may not be feasible. The grave should be clearly marked at the site and on a map. Recovery of the body should be left to professional rescue services. When death is the result of an accident, it must be reported to the police. Post-mortem examination of the body and a subsequent inquest are required by law. If death is clearly due to natural causes, for example a heart attack, the deceased's doctor may issue a death certificate. However, autopsy examination is required in most cases of sudden death on a trail or expedition.

Sudden loss of a travelling companion is a profoundly upsetting experience and the other members of the party are likely to be shocked and distressed. Efforts should be directed towards giving them support and comfort.

See also **Artificial Respiration, Hypothermia**

DEHYDRATION

In health the body loses water through the skin, the lungs and the kidneys. These losses are replaced by oral intake of fluids. A fairly accurate fluid balance is maintained through the action of the kidneys and a thirst control centre in the brain. If hot weather or heavy exertion results in profuse sweating, there is a reduction of urine output and the individual feels thirsty. This persists until the fluid lost as sweat has been replaced. Conversely, if an individual imbibes a large volume of fluid, the kidneys respond by increasing the urine output until the excess has been eliminated. This finely-tuned system is disrupted if, for some reason, normal fluid intake is interrupted or there is excessive loss of fluid, for example, as a result of diarrhoea, vomiting, sustained rapid respiration (as in pneumonia) or excessive perspiration. An individual who is running a fever is predisposed to dehydration because of drenching sweats, an increased breathing rate and often a disinclination to drink fluids.

The signs of dehydration are a dry mouth, a sunken appearance around the eyes, loss of skin elasticity and dark, concentrated urine, if indeed any is produced. As dehydration becomes more profound, the pulse becomes rapid and feeble and the breathing rate increases. The individual will sink into a coma and die if vigorous attempts at rehydration are not initiated immediately.

Severe dehydration can be avoided if fluid intake is increased during very hot weather and periods of heavy exertion. An individual with diarrhoea or pneumonia should be encouraged to swallow small volumes of fluid at frequent intervals.

Once there are definite signs of dehydration, fluid should be given by intravenous infusion if feasible. Failing this, rehydration fluid may be given frequently, but in small quantities. A suitable rehydration solution is easily prepared by adding eight level teaspoons of sugar and half a level teaspoon of salt to a litre of water.

See also **Diarrhoea, Heat Exhaustion**

DIABETES

The human body consists of millions of microscopic cells which require glucose for nourishment. This is conveyed to the cells via the bloodstream. The level of glucose in the bloodstream is accurately regulated by a number of hormones, the most important of these being insulin which is produced by the pancreas. When there is a real or relative deficiency in insulin, normal control of blood glucose is lost and a person is said to have diabetes mellitus.

Diabetes may develop slowly, over weeks, or come on acutely. The individual is continually thirsty and often hungry as well. The volume of urine increases markedly, with the need to get out of bed several times each night. There is increased susceptibility to skin and other infections and long-term the diabetic is predisposed to heart disease and nerve degeneration.

When onset of diabetes is acute, severe dehydration may develop in a matter of hours and the individual will gradually lapse into a coma with deep, sighing respiration and a very high blood sugar level. Coma of this nature may also occur in treated diabetics if daily insulin injections are omitted for some reason or a severe infection occurs.

Hyperglycaemic coma of gradual onset, over several hours or even days, must be distinguished from the rapid loss of consciousness (hypoglycaemic coma) which may occur in a diabetic who administers the prescribed insulin but then misses one or two meals or exercises excessively. As the blood sugar level drops in response to insulin and exercise, there is a feeling of faintness and dizziness accompanied by perspiration and rapid heart beat. Speedy ingestion of glucose or other carbohydrate at this stage may revive the person. Once consciousness has been lost, a subcutaneous injection of *Glucogon* or an intravenous injection of glucose is necessary to restore the blood sugar level. Individuals with established diabetes usually know a great deal about their condition and look after themselves well. They are capable of living a full and active life and need not be excluded from expeditions or long hikes – provided certain precautions are observed. Insulin should be administered as prescribed and meals eaten regularly. Food intake may need to be increased to balance increased energy expenditure.

Foot care is important and minor cuts and scratches should be treated promptly with antiseptic ointment to avoid infection. Diabetics are instructed to carry glucose cubes and a *Glucogon* injection kit with them at all times. Several glucose cubes should be consumed at the first sign of faintness or loss of energy, and followed up with a sandwich or rusk. When a diabetic is clearly unwell, steps should be taken to obtain medical help. A good intake of fluids must be ensured and insulin injections given as prescribed. It may be advisable to start an antibiotic. When signs of dehydration are present a medical emergency exists and hospital management is urgently needed.

*D*IARRHOEA

Diarrhoea is the frequent passing of loose stools. It is often preceded by colicky abdominal pain and may be associated with vomiting. The commonest cause of diarrhoea is gastro-enteritis due to viral or bacterial infection. Diarrhoea may also occur as an allergic reaction to eating certain foods, for example shell-fish. When a number of individuals all develop diarrhoea some hours after a shared meal the probable cause is food poisoning.

In most instances, diarrhoea will resolve spontaneously after a few days. However, fluid loss in the stools may be significant and steps should be taken to prevent dehydration. The afflicted person should refrain from taking solid food as this is likely to stimulate further bowel movements. Small amounts of liquid (100–150 ml) should be taken at intervals of 20–30 minutes. A suitable solution is made by adding eight level teaspoons of sugar and half a level teaspoon of salt to a litre of water. Anti-diarrhoea tablets and codeine will reduce intestinal movement and aid recovery. An antibiotic should not be taken.

The term dysentery is used for the passage of red blood and mucus in loose stools. This usually indicates infection of the large intestine with specific bacteria or amoebae. Bacterial dysentery is treated with an antibiotic and amoebiasis is treated with a drug called metronidazole. This treatment should be administered by a doctor.

See also **Dehydration, Food Poisoning, Gastro-enteritis**

DISLOCATED JOINTS

A joint is dislocated when the normal relationship between two opposing bony surfaces has been disrupted. Dislocation of a joint is commonly associated with the stretching or rupture of surrounding ligaments. There may also be damage to joint surfaces and fractures in adjacent bone. The joints most commonly dislocated include the shoulder, the hip, the ankle and the small joints of the fingers and thumb.

Some individuals suffer recurrent dislocation of a joint, particularly the shoulder, following damage to the ligaments. When this is the case a surgical operation is necessary to prevent further dislocations. The usual symptoms of a dislocation are severe pain and loss of joint function. The joint may appear deformed and will soon become swollen. Any attempt to move it through its normal range will cause extreme pain.

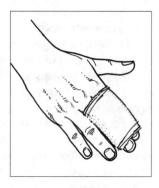

Dislocation of a finger joint can often be reduced by applying gentle traction to the distal end. The finger should then be splinted by strapping it to an adjacent finger. It is inadvisable to try to reduce dislocation of other joints; attempts will cause the victim great pain and may cause further damage to joint surfaces, fractures, obstruction or tearing of arteries and distortion of nerves, with resulting para-

lysis. The joint should be left in the position which causes least discomfort and bound with a crêpe bandage. A pain-killing drug should be administered and the patient transported to hospital for X-ray examination and formal reduction under anaesthetic. Immobilize the joint for up to two weeks to allow full healing.

See also **Ankle Injuries, Fractures**

DROWNING

Death from drowning is due to oxygen deprivation. About 80% of all drowning victims are found with their lungs filled with water. The remainder develop a reflex spasm of the vocal cords which prevents water and air entering the lungs. Death in these cases is a result of asphyxia.

There are many recorded cases of survival after prolonged immersion, particularly in very cold water. Thus, attempts at resuscitating a 'drowned' person should not be abandoned until there is no doubt that the subject is dead.

The first treatment priority is to get the individual out of the water and to start mouth-to-mouth ventilation immediately. In certain circumstances, for example when the victim is far from the shore, ventilation should be started as soon as the head can be raised above water.

An attempt should be made to locate the neck pulse (carotid). If this is absent, external cardiac massage must be started and co-ordinated with artificial respiration. If other rescuers are present, wet clothing should be removed, and the individual dried and covered with blankets. Cardiac massage should not cease until a spontaneous carotid pulse is felt. Ventilation must continue until spontaneous respiration resumes.

If feasible, there should be rapid transfer to hospital, where resuscitation can be continued. Attempts to resuscitate a drowned person should continue as long as his or her body temperature is below normal. Death may be assumed only if there are no signs of life despite body temperature in the normal range.

See also **Artificial Respiration, Asphyxiation, Hypothermia**

DRUG OVERDOSE

A drug overdose may be accidental or intentional. Children under the age of five may find and ingest tablets and medicines in the course of their exploratory play – often with serious and even fatal consequences. Adults may confuse containers in the dark and accidentally ingest the wrong tablets or fluid. This seldom has serious consequences unless the substance swallowed is very poisonous, for example an organophosphate insecticide. Adults and children who intentionally overdose with drugs or poisonous substances are emotionally disturbed or severely depressed and have suicide in mind.

The effects of drug overdose depends on the drug taken. A large overdose of paracetamol will cause liver damage; certain anti-depressants cause heart toxicity; anti-convulsant and anti-anxiety drugs cause unsteadiness and sedation followed by coma.

It is important to establish *which* and *how much* of a drug has been taken. This can often be done by examining containers.

If the subject is fully conscious, vomiting can sometimes be induced by pushing two fingers down the throat. This should *not* be attempted if the subject is drowsy or unconscious as vomitus may be inhaled. If signs of shock are present, the feet should be elevated above the level of the trunk and mouth-to-mouth ventilation instituted if respiration fails. If the drug is known and there is access to communication systems, information can be obtained about specific management from a Poisons Information Centre. Urgent transfer to a medical facility is advisable in all cases except those in which the amount ingested is very small.

See also **Artificial Respiration, Poison Centres, Poisonous Plants, Shock**

*E*AR INJURIES & INFECTIONS

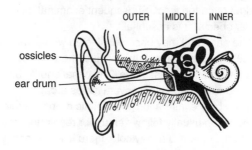

The external ear consists of cartilage and a little fat covered by skin. The *outer* ear passage ends in a very sensitive membrane known as the ear drum. Beyond this lies the *middle* ear cavity which contains three tiny bones (ossicles) linked to each other in series. Sound waves cause vibrations of the ear drum and these are transmitted by the ossicles to the *inner* ear where they are converted to nerve impulses. These nerve impulses travel to the brain and are interpreted as sounds. A narrow drainage tube, the eustachian tube, connects the middle ear with the back of the throat.

The external ear may be cut, torn or even severed from the head. Bleeding can be controlled by local pressure. Plastic surgery may be necessary, and severed portions should not be discarded if medical assistance is close at hand (*see* Amputation).

Extreme irritation will be experienced if an insect or tick finds its way into the ear passage. If it cannot be dislodged with a finger, the ear canal should be filled with water, preferably slightly warmed. The offending insect should float to the surface and can be removed.

The ear drum may be perforated when a sharp object penetrates the ear. It may also be perforated by a sudden, very loud noise, for example a nearby explosion. There will be sharp pain, bleeding and some loss of hearing. The ear should be washed gently and the external opening plugged with a pledget of cotton wool. Subsequent examination by an ear specialist is essential.

The ear canal may become infected with a variety of bacterial organisms. If this occurs, there will be irritation and some discharge. The canal should be mopped with cotton wool several times a day, followed by the instillation of antibiotic drops. Middle ear infection usually follows an upper respiratory tract infection, such as a heavy cold; there is acute pain in the ear and some loss of hearing. Untreated, the ear drum may rupture and discharge pus down the canal. This can be treated with an antibiotic and pain-killers.

See also **Amputation, Bleeding**

*E*LECTRIC SHOCK

The effect of an electric shock ranges from momentary pain to immediate respiratory arrest and death. The severity of the reaction is determined by the magnitude of the current, duration of contact, moistness of the skin, the distance travelled by the current through the body to the ground, and the nature of the surface underfoot. Standing on a wet surface or in water increases susceptibility to electrical injury.

Electric energy is converted to heat as it passes through the skin, and results in severe burns. High tension current causes immediate respiratory arrest and cardiac standstill. Lesser currents may induce ventricular fibrillation (*see* Heart Attack). The heart may resume its normal beat when the current stops. Electricity may also cause extensive damage to the brain, spinal cord and peripheral nerves.

Electric shock is possible from faulty camp generators, electrical appliances, and fallen or excavated high tension cables. Lightning strike may occur during electrical storms.

Immediately after a severe shock, the casualty will be unconscious and not breathing. The first priority is to break contact with the source of current by switching off the appliance or, if this is not possible, pushing the source, for example a cable, away from the victim with a wooden pole, plank or other insulator material. The victim must *not* be touched until this has been done. Thereafter immediately institute mouth-to-mouth respiration and, if there is no discernible pulse in the neck, start external cardiac compression. Persist with attempts at resuscitation for at least an hour as recovery from electric shock may occur even after prolonged cardio respiratory standstill. It may be necessary to continue cardiac compression and assist ventilation during transfer to hospital. Electric burns should be covered with dry dressings.

See also **Artificial Respiration, Asphyxiation, Burns and Scalds, Heart Attack, Shock, Unconsciousness**

*E*PILEPSY

The term 'epilepsy' means a tendency to have recurrent convulsions or seizures. Epilepsy may occur as a manifestation of long-standing brain damage. It may also occur in individuals who have no structural brain abnormality.

Epilepsy can be controlled with anti-convulsant drugs. If these are taken regularly as prescribed, seizure control is excellent in about 70% of persons with epilepsy. They are able to lead a full, normal life and need not be debarred from mountain climbing, hiking trails or expeditions. When seizure control is incomplete, however, the individual should not go swimming alone and rock climbing may be inadvisable. A seizure may be brought on by fatigue, extreme hunger, anxiety or a viral infection. For further detail and the management of individual convulsions, *see* Convulsions.

EYE INJURIES

Grains of sand, vegetable matter or any other small object which sticks to the front of the eye or gets under an eyelid will cause intense irritation and discomfort. Tears will flow and the eye will be held tightly closed. If the foreign matter remains in the eye for

any length of time, the surface of the cornea may become ulcerated. This causes persistent pain and irritation.

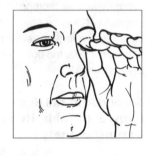

To remove a foreign body, the eyelids should be opened and the eye examined in a good light. It is usually possible to

see the foreign body stuck to the front surface of the eye. It may, however, be lodged under the upper eyelid. If this is the case, place the tip of your index finger on the middle of the eyelid, and with the index finger and thumb of the other hand gently pull downwards on the eyelashes. Slight pressure with the

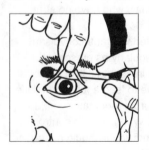

84

index finger will invert the upper eyelid and its under-surface can then be inspected. Another way of inverting the upper eyelid is to use a match, as illustrated. A foreign body can often be removed with the corner of a clean handkerchief or other soft material. If this cannot be achieved it is advisable to seek medical help. The surface of the eye may have to be anaesthetized before the foreign body is lifted off with a fine instrument. Corneal ulceration may take several days to heal and there is the danger of infection. Antibiotic drops should be used, and the eye kept covered for 24 hours after removal of the foreign body.

A blow to the eye may cause a haemorrhage into the eyeball, dislocation of the lens and detachment of the retina. Penetrating injury will lacerate the cornea or sclera and can result in infection; damage may also be done to the lens and retina. The injured eye should be covered with a pad of soft material and bandaged lightly. A pain-killing drug and an antibiotic should be administered if available. The casualty

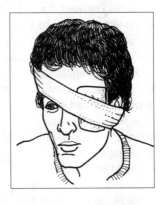

should be kept at rest and transported to hospital as quickly as possible. If a chemical or other potentially harmful fluid is splashed into the eye, it should be washed repeatedly with water until all irritation has ceased. Significant eye injuries require specialist treatment if any vision is to be preserved. When one eye has been severely damaged there is always the risk of loss of vision in the other eye by a process called sympathetic ophthalmia.

See also **Blindness**

FACE & NOSE INJURIES

Even relatively minor facial injuries may bleed profusely as the face has a rich blood supply. It is important to determine whether an injury involves only superficial skin and soft tissues or extends to underlying bone, sinuses and nerves. Severe facial injury with multiple bone fractures may cause airway obstruction. Bleeding into the eye sockets may produce pressure effects which cause double vision. Jaw fractures may disrupt tooth alignment and make chewing impossible and swallowing difficult.

The first priority in severe facial injury is to ensure that the casualty has a clear airway – either through the mouth or nose. It may be necessary to remove blood clot and to insert a piece of tubing through the nose or mouth. Bleeding is arrested by direct pressure with a pad or cloth, taking care not to displace further broken nasal, cheek and facial bones. Once the bleeding has stopped, dressings should be applied and kept in place with bandages.

A fractured jaw may be supported by passing a bandage under the chin and securing it over the crown of the head. It is inadvisable to attempt suturing of facial wounds in the field as cosmetic results may be unsatisfactory. If bleeding has

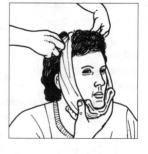

been extensive, an intravenous infusion should be set up. A strong pain-killer may be given if there has been no loss of consciousness. The casualty must be evacuated to hospital. The edges of minor facial cuts may be approximated with sticking plaster. Nose bleeding is arrested by squeezing the nose firmly between the finger and thumb for several minutes.

FAINTING

Fainting occurs when there is a temporary decrease in the arterial blood supply to the brain. The individual, who is usually standing or sitting, becomes extremely pale and then falls to the ground unconscious. There may be a few jerky movements of the limbs, and if the bladder happens to be full, control may be lost. Consciousness returns within seconds of reaching a horizontal position, although the person may feel weak and unsteady for some time and have a distressing headache.

Fainting is often related to illnesses such as influenza and gastro-enteritis. Low blood sugar may be a precipitating factor in someone who has missed meals or is dieting. Fainting can also occur after prolonged standing in hot or poorly ventilated surroundings, as a result of sudden severe pain, or sudden emotional shock.

Fainting must be distinguished from other causes of sudden loss of consciousness such as convulsions and stroke. Identifying features are preceding dizziness and discomfort, extreme pallor, a weak or absent wrist pulse on falling down, and rapid return to consciousness. An individual who is about to faint may feel light-headed, nauseous and dizzy. There may be abdominal discomfort, sweating and awareness of the heart beat. All these symptoms precede loss of consciousness.

When a convulsion occurs, loss of consciousness is sudden and total, although in some cases there may be a warning aura of strange feelings. The face is often suffused during a convulsion and the pulse strong. In the case of a stroke, full consciousness may not return for many hours, and there is often impairment of speech and limb movement.

A person who has fainted should be kept lying down in the shade until there is a strong pulse at the wrist and he or she is feeling much better. Excessive and/or tight clothing should be removed. A drink of cold water is usually appreciated, as is sponging of the face. Exertion should be avoided until there has been full recovery.

See also **Convulsions, Stroke**

*F*EVER

In a healthy state, body temperature is kept in the narrow range between 35,5°C and 37°C. A fine balance is maintained between heat loss (*see* Hypothermia) and heat production through body metabolism and exertion. Defence mechanisms against harmful bacteria and viruses function best at body temperature above the normal range, and so when infection occurs, a fever develops. Specialized defence cells initiate the release of a chain of chemicals which increase heat production and diminish heat loss, for instance by causing constriction of blood vessels in the skin.

An individual with fever will usually feel unwell. There is a chilly sensation of the skin which may be followed by teeth chattering and shivering.

Headache, generalized muscle aches, backache and joint pains are common, and a fever blister may develop on the lip. Delirium – wandering of the mind and incoherent speech – sometimes occurs with high fever, and certain young children (usually under the age of five) are prone to convulsions.

Fever in a previously healthy individual is a response to an infection, and treatment must be directed at the infection. Other symptoms may indicate the nature and site of the infection.

For example, with typhoid the fever rises higher each evening until a plateau is reached, while fever which recurs on alternate days or every third day suggests certain forms of malaria. A drop in body temperature and relief from the symptoms which accompany fever can be achieved in a number of ways. Tepid sponging is effective, particularly if this can be combined with fanning.

Aspirin and paracetamol will lower the temperature and are both effective against headache, muscle pains and general discomfort. If a fever persists for several days and the cause is not self-evident, it is advisable to seek medical advice.

Aspirin should not be given to young children as it may induce serious illness.

FOOD POISONING

Food poisoning occurs in a number of ways:

■ Normal foodstuffs become contaminated with bacteria, toxins or chemicals.
■ Foods undergo changes which render them toxic.
■ Poisonous substances are eaten by mistake.

Bacterial food poisoning occurs after eating infected meat, chicken and dairy products which have been precooked and improperly stored. Certain strains of bacteria produce a toxin which causes rapid onset of symptoms. Unwashed fruit and vegetables may be contaminated with insecticide spray. Decomposition in the tissue of normally edible fish may render it toxic, and shellfish contaminated with organisms (red tide) can cause severe symptoms. Poisonous mushrooms provide the best example of an intrinsically toxic substance which may be eaten by mistake.

The incubation period after ingestion of contaminated food varies from 3–48 hours. Abdominal pain, diarrhoea and vomiting are the usual symptoms. These resolve within 24–36 hours when a toxin is responsible, but may persist for longer if there has been bacterial infection. Insecticide contamination causes symptoms of organophosphate poisoning (*see* Poisoning). Fish poisoning (scombroid) causes diarrhoea, flushing, sweating and dizziness and may be followed by skin rash and facial swelling.

Shellfish poisoning causes a tingling sensation in face and limbs, followed by dizziness and unsteadiness. In severe cases, muscle paralysis may result. Mushroom poisoning causes diarrhoea, vomiting and abdominal pain, followed by progressive liver failure.

In most cases, food poisoning will resolve spontaneously. The victim should rest and not take solid food until diarrhoea and vomiting have stopped. Small volumes of rehydration fluid should be drunk frequently. *Imodium* or codeine will provide some relief from abdominal cramps. If severe vomiting and diarrhoea lead to dehydration, an intravenous drip should be set up. Scombroid poisoning resolves spontaneously in a matter of hours. However, individuals with suspected mushroom poisoning require urgent hospital attention.

Poisoning can be prevented by careful attention to food storage and preparation.

■ Perishable foodstuffs should be kept in a refrigerator or cool box.
■ Cooked food should be eaten soon after preparation as cooking temperatures destroy bacteria.
■ Pre-cooking and storing food should be avoided
■ Individuals with infected skin lesions should be excluded from food preparation.
■ Avoid eating fish which is not absolutely fresh.
■ Wild mushrooms should never be eaten unless they have been identified as an edible species.

See also **Dehydration, Diarrhoea, Gastro-enteritis, Poisoning**

FRACTURES

A healthy bone will break (fracture) only when subjected to a strong direct or twisting force. The bones of elderly people are more brittle and a relatively minor fall may result in a fracture.

The signs of a fracture are deformity, extreme pain aggravated by movement, swelling and shock. Sometimes the grating of bone ends against each other can be heard (crepitus). Fractures are always associated with some blood loss into the surrounding tissues. In the case of a thigh bone fracture this concealed bleeding may be considerable and aggravate shock.

Any movement of the injured area will cause acute pain. The subject should be kept at complete rest and supported in the position found to be most comfortable. If a strong pain-killer is available this

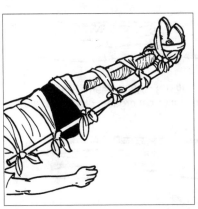

should be administered well before any attempt is made to splint the affected bone. Fractures in the upper limbs are immobilized by strapping the arm to the front of the chest. Lower limb fractures are splinted by tying the legs together. An outside splint of wood may be used, if available, but this should be well padded to avoid further discomfort. If signs of shock are present an intravenous infusion should be set up, if this is feasible.

There are five types of fracture:

◼ Closed (simple) fracture – the surrounding skin is intact and bacteria do not have direct access to the broken skin.

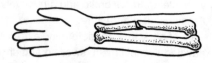

◼ Compound (open) fracture – an associated skin wound through which bone ends may protrude.

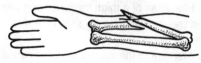

◼ Comminuted fracture – the bone is broken into more than two fragments.

◼ Complicated fracture – bone fragments have caused damage to internal organs, blood vessels or nerves.

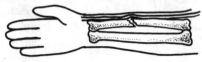

◼ Greenstick fractures – the bone is cracked and bent but remains intact. (This type of fracture occurs only in children.)

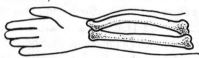

FROSTBITE

When exposed to cold conditions the body conserves heat by reducing blood flow to the skin. This is most marked in the hands and feet, which will feel cold and numb. If the temperature continues to drop, blood flow in these extremities ceases altogether, and water in the body cells freezes. This is called frostbite. Permanent cell damage and death of tissue (gangrene) can occur if the induvidual's circulation is not quickly restored.

Frostbite is likely to occur at high altitude, in snow and ice conditions, and during extreme inland winter conditions, particularly if there is a wind blowing. It can be avoided by wearing appropriate clothing – thick woollen socks, sturdy boots, gloves and outer mittens, a balaclava or other protection for the ears and face, in addition to heavy-weight underwear, sweaters, anorak and an outer windproof jacket. Fingers and toes should be exercised at intervals. Alcohol and smoking should be avoided during exposure to extreme cold: smoking causes constriction of blood vessels and can aggravate frostbite. Alcohol dilates blood vessels in the skin and so increases heat loss. A hand which begins to feel cold should be warmed by holding it in the opposite armpit.

Frostbitten tissue appears greyish-white and feels cold and hard to the touch. Initially there may be pain, but later the area becomes numb, and the feeling of cold and pain disappears. In severe cases, frostbite

extends to muscles and deep tissues. Attempts should be made to place the frozen area against warm body tissue. For example, hands can be warmed in the armpits or against the side of the chest, and a foot can be warmed either in the armpit or against the warm stomach of a companion!

A frostbite victim should be taken to shelter as quickly as possible. The frostbitten part should be immersed in water at a temperature of ±40°C, that is, slightly higher than body temperature, until normal circulation and sensation has returned. Rubbing, hot water bottles and sitting next to a stove or fire should be avoided as these may increase tissue damage. In severe cases, it may be many days before the full extent of frostbite can be assessed. Amputation and plastic surgery may be necessary.

See also **Hypothermia**

GASTRO-ENTERITIS

Gastro-enteritis is caused by viral or bacterial infection of the stomach and small intestine. Organisms responsible for the condition are spread from case to case via contaminated foodstuffs, drinking water and eating utensils. The most prominent symptoms are vomiting, colicky abdominal pain and watery diarrhoea. The affected person is not usually feverish but feels weak and listless. Severe vomiting and diarrhoea will lead to dehydration unless steps are taken to prevent this.

Most attacks of gastro-enteritis are self-limited and last no longer than 48 hours. The affected person should refrain from taking solid foods. Small amounts of fluid should be taken at frequent intervals as severe vomiting and diarrhoea may lead to dehydration. Anti-diarrhoea tablets and codeine will relieve abdominal discomfort and reduce the loss of body fluids. If signs of dehydration do appear, an intravenous infusion may be necessary. Gastro-enteritis can be fatal in young children, and medical assistance is advisable at an early stage.

Gastro-enteritis can be avoided by maintaining good standards of hygiene. When there is any possibility of contamination, drinking water should be boiled, filtered or chemically treated. Those with gastro-enteritis should not be involved in food preparation. Every fixed camp should have an adequate latrine well away from the source of water, and cooking and living areas.

See also **Dehydration, Diarrhoea, Food Poisoning**

GUNSHOT WOUNDS

Gunshot wounds are almost always of a serious nature. When the chest has been penetrated there may be serious damage to the heart, lungs and major blood vessels. A wound in the abdomen is likely to cause multiple intestinal perforations, major bleeding and damage to the liver, kidney and bladder. When a high velocity bullet strikes a limb it is likely to cause comminuted fractures of the bone as well as soft tissue injury and bleeding.

Internal haemorrhage and shock are the immediate dangers. Make the casualty feel comfortable with the legs raised slightly above the level of the head and trunk. However, if the casualty experiences breathing difficulties he or she may feel more comfortable in a semi-sitting position.

Control external bleeding by applying direct pressure with a dressing, towel or clean cloth. Entry and exit wounds should be covered with simple dry dressings. If available, a strong pain-killer should be administered. Nothing should be taken by mouth if

the abdomen has been pierced, and the casualty
should be transported to hospital as quickly as possible for specialist treatment.

See also **Abdominal Injuries, Bleeding, Chest
Injuries, Head Injuries, Shock**

Head Injuries

Head injuries vary in severity from superficial cuts
and bruises to severe brain damage with intracranial
haemorrhage. The scalp has a rich blood supply and
profuse bleeding may result from a relatively small
wound. A head injury should be regarded as serious
if there has been *any* period of unconsciousness,
and very serious if there is a return to unconsciousness after a period of regained consciousness. Other
serious signs include a pulse rate below 60, unequal
pupils, sluggish pupil response to light, bleeding from
the ears, and watery discharge from the nose or ears.
    A clear airway must be established if the casualty
is unconscious. Nothing should be given by mouth.
It is usually advisable to keep the person horizontal,
with the head slightly higher than the feet. If, however,
there has been considerable external blood loss, or if
signs of shock are present, the feet should be elevated. An intravenous infusion should be set up if possible. Bleeding from scalp wounds can always be
stopped by direct pressure. Once bleeding has been
halted, the dressing can be secured with a bandage.
The casualty's pulse, pupils and level of consciousness must be carefully monitored. A slow pulse,
abnormal pupils and deteriorating level of consciousness indicate intracranial haemorrhage and/or brain
swelling. Urgent hospital treatment will be required.

See also **Bleeding, Concussion, Shock,
Unconsciousness**

HEART ATTACK

The heart is a highly specialized muscle which pumps arterial blood to all parts of the body and venous blood to the lungs. The heart muscle itself is supplied by two arteries, called coronary arteries, which branch from the aorta at its origin from the heart. The rate of heart contraction is regulated according to the body's needs under changing circumstances. At rest it is slow; during strenuous exercise there is a marked increase in rate and cardiac contraction becomes more forceful.

Acute heart attacks usually take one of two forms. One form occurs when a coronary artery becomes blocked and the sector of heart muscle which it supplies is deprived of oxygen and nutrients. This muscle tissue suffers damage and will die if the blood supply is not rapidly restored. The victim experiences sudden crushing pain in the centre of the chest, which may radiate up into the neck and down the left arm. There is sweating, pallor and collapse. The wrist pulse may be absent or weak and feeble. Shortness of breath is often a prominent symptom. If the area of damaged muscle is extensive, effective cardiac contraction is no longer possible. The victim will lose consciousness and die.

The other common form of heart attack occurs when there is a sudden loss of the heart's natural rhythm. The normal, regular beat is replaced by rapid, incomplete contractions (ventricular fibrillation) which are ineffective at circulating arterial blood. Impaired blood supply to the brain causes rapid loss of consciousness. The victim becomes very pale and no pulse can be felt in the neck or at the wrist. Death occurs after a few minutes unless the heartbeat can be restored.

An individual experiencing sudden severe chest pain must be placed at complete rest in a horizontal position. If, however, there is marked shortness of breath, a semi-sitting position may be more comfortable. Pain relief is the first priority. If an injectable pain-killer is available, this should be administered; if not, some relief may be obtained from codeine. Further management will depend on the availability of skilled medical care. The patient should be comforted and kept at complete rest while plans for hospitalization are made.

If there is a sudden loss of consciousness and no perceptible heart beat, suspect ventricular fibrillation. Give the front of the chest one or two forceful thumps with the side of a fisted hand. This is sometimes sufficient to restore normal rhythm. If no response is gained, external cardiac massage must be initiated.

■ Place the individual in a supine position on a firm surface.

■ Kneel next to him/her and place the heel of the right hand at the lower end of the breast bone. Interlock the fingers of the left hand.

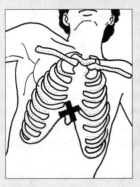

■ Press down forcefully. This will compress the heart between the breast bone and the spinal column, and force blood into the arteries. Apply this pressure in a regular sequence at a rate of 60 compressions per minute.

As breathing ceases when the heart stops, it is usually necessary to combine artificial ventilation with heart massage. When resuscitation is being carried out by two people, the one engaged in cardiac massage should pause for a moment after every fourth compression to allow the other person to inflate the chest. When there is only one person available, he or she should compress the chest ten times and then inflate the lungs twice, before resuming cardiac compression. Heart-lung resuscitation should continue until a spontaneous heartbeat and respiration return, or the victim is pronounced dead.

See also **Artificial Respiration, Chest Pain, Pneumonia, Shock**

HEAT EXHAUSTION

In environmental conditions of heat and high humidity, body temperature is kept within the normal range (35–37°C) by increased blood flow to the skin and sweating. Sweating is effective in lowering body temperature only as long as water evaporates from the skin and hydration remains good. On a hot day, under conditions of heavy exertion, a litre of sweat may be lost every hour. If this fluid is not replaced and exertion continues, dehydration results. There will be a loss of thirst and a rapid rise in body temperature, followed by loss of consciousness.

The term 'heat stroke' is used when there is total failure of normal heat regulation mechanisms: sweating ceases and there may be convulsions and coma. Some 60% of such cases are fatal.

It is important to ascertain the availability of drinking water before embarking on any hike or climb in hot or humid weather. If no surface water is available, every member of the party should carry one to two litres of water (the daily ration). Each person should wear a hat and appropriate lightweight clothing, and remember to take precautions against sunburn. The party should rest at regular intervals and each member should aim to drink at least one cup of water (150 ml) every hour.

The severity of exertion should be related to fitness and age. Unfit and older individuals are not advised to walk or climb in very hot weather with those who are young and supremely fit. Care should be taken not to overextend children. Individuals who become stranded in very hot conditions should walk only at night and seek shelter during the day. If possible, a sleeping surface should be constructed above the ground level as this will be cooler.

Suspect heat exhaustion on a hot day if a member of the party becomes uncharacteristically quiet or seems to be falling behind. Rambling incoherence and collapse are serious signs. Try to get the individual into shade *immediately,* remove clothing (within reason), bathe with cool water (if available), and fan. If the person is conscious, encourage him or her to swallow small quantities of water at intervals of a few minutes. Don't move on until he or she is fully revived. If consciousness is impaired, do not move beyond the nearest shady spot. Arrange transport to hospital as soon as possible.

See also **Dehydration**

HYPOTHERMIA

The human body loses heat in five ways:

◼ By radiation to surrounding colder objects.
◼ By conduction to surfaces with which there is direct contact, such as the ground.
◼ By warming cold air breathed into the lungs.
◼ By evaporation of moisture from wet clothes.

■ By convection – warming the layer of air immediately surrounding the body. (If this layer of air is constantly replaced – the situation which arises whenever a breeze is blowing – loss of heat by convection can be enormous. For example, when the air temperature is 0°C a wind velocity of 25 km per hour, a moderate breeze, will rapidly drop the temperature of exposed skin to −12° with a profoundly chilling effect on the whole body.)

Hypothermia is avoided by adopting the following sensible practices:

■ Do not start out on a climb, hike or trail in the face of obviously deteriorating weather.
■ However warm the day may seem, *never* set out without a warm sweater, an anorak and a pair of long trousers in your backpack.
■ On any long hike, maintain a steady intake of food as this will ensure constant production of body heat.
■ If caught in bad weather, seek shelter early and, in particular, get out of the wind before wind chill and exhaustion take their toll. It is far better to conserve body heat by huddling together behind a rock than to dissipate it by continuing in a gale until hypothermia induces total collapse and probable death.

When a person's body temperature drops below 34°C the ability to shiver is lost. The victim feels very tired, is disorientated and may act in an illogical manner. Speech becomes slurred, co-ordination is impaired, muscle strength is lost, and there is an overwhelming desire to sleep. As body temperature drops further, consciousness is lost, breathing becomes slow and shallow, and the heartbeat becomes irregular and increasingly difficult to detect. A victim of hypothermia must be moved to shelter as quickly as possible. Protection from wind is essential, and all exertion must be avoided as this promotes further heat loss. Wet clothing must be removed and replaced with dry garments. Rewarming cannot occur without external provision of heat. Place the individual in a sleeping bag in front of a fire. If no fire is available, another warm individual should get into the sleeping bag with the victim. If conscious, give the victim warm, sweet fluids to drink. In a tent or hut, warm the air breathed in by lighting stoves.

Move the victim very gently at all times as rough handling may precipitate heart irregularities. If breathing has stopped and there is no perceptible heartbeat, cardiac compression and mouth-to-mouth ventilation must be instituted and continued until spontaneous action returns, or there is still no sign of life after the body has been re-warmed. No hypothermia victim should be pronounced dead until 'warm and dead'.

See also **Frostbite, Heart Attack**

*H*YSTERIA

An individual who is extremely anxious or under severe emotional stress may experience symptoms which are identical to those caused by a physical disease. Palpitations and chest pain may suggest heart disease; colicky abdominal pain may raise suspicion of kidney stones, gall bladder disease or even appendicitis and limb weakness may mimic a stroke. The symptoms are very real to the individual, but a careful observer may notice certain inconsistencies and incongruities: the sufferer looks rested and calm despite the severity of reported symptoms; a good appetite is maintained; fever and vomiting are seldom features; normal movements return to the 'paralysed' limb when attention is focused elsewhere. Friendly conversation may reveal sources of stress and causes for anxiety in the individual's personal environment. On a long trail or expedition he or she may feel unequal to the physical demands being made, or be anxious about real or imagined dangers.

It is important to be reasonably certain that the individual does not have a serious disease. Once this has been established, treatment should be supportive and reassuring. Where possible, the individual should be relieved of tasks and duties which give rise to stress. Anxieties should be discussed and analysed in a rational manner and, if possible, dispelled. This type of approach will usually be followed by gradual resolution of the symptoms.

Hysterical reactions should be distinguished from malingering. The malingerer deliberately reports a symptom or feigns a disorder to avoid some activity or task regarded as unattractive, but is fully aware of the deception and motive for it.

INSECT STINGS AND BITES

Insects abound in the southern African countryside, and a number of species deliver stings or bites which can be harmful to human beings. Wasp stings are

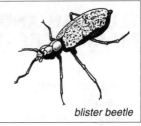

blister beetle

painful, as are the bites of certain ants. Local skin reactions may develop, but generalized hypersensitivity reactions are extremely uncommon. Flea and bug bites cause itchy local reactions and small, scattered blisters (papular urticaria) in sensitive subjects. Serious diseases, such as typhus

rove beetle

and bubonic plague, may be transmitted by fleas which pass from infected rats to human beings. Blister beetles, when threatened in any way, release a fluid which is highly irritant and poisonous; skin contact causes blistering. Accidental ingestion of one of these beetles can be fatal. If this happens, induce vomiting (*see* Poisoning). The tiny rove beetle sometimes finds its way into people's eyes. It too produces a toxin which is highly irritant. Contact with the bristles of certain caterpillars can cause burning local skin irritation and mild blistering.

Local application of calamine lotion or a soothing antihistamine is usually sufficient to provide symptomatic relief. There is, however, always some danger of secondary infection and a check should be kept on spreading inflammation and painful glands in the armpits or groin. An insect in the eye should be removed, and the eye rinsed with water.

See also **Bee Stings, Malaria, Poisoning, Scorpion Stings, Spiders, Tick-bite Fever**

JELLY-FISH AND OTHER MARINE CREATURES

Venoms toxic to man are produced by a number of marine creatures. Contact with a jelly-fish, for example, induces symptoms which range from burning discomfort to severe pain, swelling and a rash. Swimmers who become entangled in the tentacles of a bluebottle (Portuguese man o'war), experience severe pain, and develop redness and swelling at the

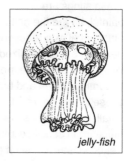
jelly-fish

points of contact. If the tentacles remain in contact with the skin for any length of time, nausea, vomiting, chills and weakness may develop; respiratory failure and death have also been reported.

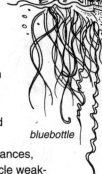
bluebottle

The sharp spines of the sea urchin can penetrate skin to a considerable depth and are extremely difficult to extract. The spines are tipped with venom which causes severe pain and, in some instances,

sea urchin

muscle weakness and breathing difficulty.

The snails which inhabit cone shells are equipped with teeth through

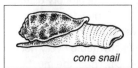
cone snail

which a powerful venom is injected. Symptoms range from a mild stinging sensation to headache, stomach cramps and potential breathing difficulties.

The octopus has a parrot-like beak which it uses to shred the marine creatures on which it lives. Salivary glands secrete a venom which is injected as the octopus bites. When a person is bitten by an octopus, symptoms range from mild discomfort to severe pain with

octopus

catfish

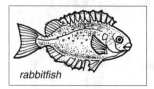

rabbitfish

firefish

stonefish

swelling, inflammation, bleeding and dizziness.

Other sea creatures which secrete venom are the stingray, eel catfish, rabbitfish, scorpionfish, firefish and stonefish.

The stingray uses its tail to inject venom; the others all have venom-bearing spines.

The most severe reaction occurs on contact with a stonefish: there is severe pain with local inflammation and numbness; nausea, vomiting, convulsions and respiratory distress may follow.

The venom of marine creatures is inactivated by very hot water (60°C). Thus, the most effective first aid measure is to immerse the affected area in the hottest water that the victim can tolerate, and maintain this for several minutes. Once the pain has been relieved, mercurochrome or antiseptic ointment should be applied to prevent secondary infection. If sea urchin spines are not easily removed, they should be left to discharge spontaneously. Avoid rubbing. In rare instances of collapse and respiratory arrest, artificial ventilation must be instituted.

See also **Artificial Respiration, Poisoning**

KIDNEY STONES

Kidney stones are formed by deposition within the kidney of substances normally carried, in solution, in the urine. A stone may be present for many years and grow to considerable size without symptoms, or it may cause recurrent urinary tract infection. The most dramatic manifestation is renal colic, which occurs when a small stone passes down the ureter (the tube connecting the kidney to the bladder). The individual experiences agonizing colicky pain, which begins in the lower back or side and radiates to the lower part of the abdomen and genitals. The pain may last only a matter of minutes or persist for several hours. It ceases once the stone has passed into the bladder but there may be some residual tenderness on the affected side of the abdomen. A burning sensation is often experienced on urination, and there is usually a little blood present in the urine.

Pain relief is the most urgent need, and is best achieved with a strong, injectable pain-killer; paracetamol and codeine are seldom sufficient. A good flow of urine should be achieved by drinking large volumes of water and other fluids. Once tenderness has subsided, the individual can resume normal activities. However, it is advisable to consult a doctor, for further investigations and possible treatment.

LEECHES

Leeches are segmented worms which live in water. They vary in length (3–18 cm) and have the ability to change shape; they have suckers at both ends, which they use to cling to a plant or animal host. They feed on sap or blood, and an anti-clotting agent is injected to promote the easy flow of blood. The bite is painless, and the victim's attention is usually first

drawn to the leech by a stream of blood running down a limb. It is traditional to encourage the leech to let go by applying a lighted match to its tail, but if a match is not readily available, it can usually be prised off.

Bleeding can be arrested by maintaining firm pressure over the site of the bite for several minutes. It is advisable to apply mercurochrome or an antiseptic ointment once the bleeding has stopped.

MALARIA

Malaria occurs in Northern Natal, the Eastern and Northern Transvaal and latitudes further north. Cases have also been reported from certain areas in the far Northern Cape.

It is a disease of hot weather and good surface water conditions where mosquitoes abound.

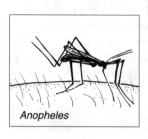

Anopheles

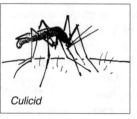

Culicid

The malaria parasite is injected into the blood stream by the bite of an Anopheles mosquito and multiplies within the red blood cells. After an incubation period of 7–14 days there is loss of energy, headache, muscle pains and vomiting. The individual feels cold and shivers (rigors). This is followed by high fever and severe sweating. Episodes of rigors, fever and sweating will recur at intervals of 1–3 days. Untreated, malaria carries a significant mortality. Serious complications include coma (cerebral malaria), renal failure and even general collapse.

Malaria should be suspected whenever weariness, headache and fever develop in a malaria area. Diagnosis is made by examination of a blood smear. When this is not feasible, however, and there is no other obvious explanation for the symptoms, it is advisable to treat for malaria. Chloroquine is the drug most widely used; quinine is also extremely effective, and may be combined with chloroquine. In areas where the parasite has become resistant to chloroquine, mefloquine is recommended.

Malaria can be avoided by taking appropriate precautions. An anti-malarial drug should be taken daily or weekly, as prescribed, from the day of entry into a malaria area, and for six weeks after leaving it. It is important to determine that the prevalent malaria parasite (for example, *Plasmodium falciparum*) is not resistant to the drug being taken. Other precautions include the wearing of long-sleeved garments and long trousers in the evenings, when mosquitoes are active, the application of mosquito repellent cream or spray, and sleeping under adequate sleeping nets.

MOUNTAIN SICKNESS

The human body functions best at sea level in a temperate climate. Good function at high altitude is possible only after certain adaptations have occurred (acclimatization). An individual, normally resident at sea level, who ascends above 3 000 metres may experience various symptoms. These include headache, nausea, breathlessness on slight exertion, palpitations, undue fatigue and a feeling of 'heaviness' in the muscles. All these symptoms will subside in the course of the first week as the body acclimatizes to the lower oxygen pressure. There are two more serious forms of mountain sickness, but these are seldom seen in southern Africa because of the absence of really high mountains (over 5 000 metres).

Congestion of the lungs (high-altitude pulmonary oedema) causes extreme breathlessness, a dry hacking cough, chest pain and palpitations. Congestion of the brain (high-altitude cerebral oedema) causes very severe headache, vomiting, visual disturbance and a staggering walk. Both conditions can be fatal, and it is essential that the victim move to a lower altitude as quickly as possible.

Mountain sickness can be avoided by ascending to high altitudes in planned stages, by avoiding over-exertion for the first few days at a new altitude, and by taking plenty of rest. The acclimatization process is enhanced by taking an acetazolamide tablet (*Diamox*), morning and evening. This will increase the flow of urine and so counteract fluid retention. Try to spend nights at the lowest altitude consistent with the climbing programme and objectives. A climber who continues to experience unpleasant symptoms after three or four days should descend to a lower altitude and allow symptoms to subside.

PNEUMONIA

Lung tissue contains many millions of microscopic air-filled chambers (alveoli). Fine capillaries are present in the walls of each chamber and as blood passes along these, oxygen is taken up and carbon dioxide released. The act of breathing replaces oxygen in the alveoli and removes carbon dioxide.

When pneumonia develops, all the alveoli in a segment or lobe of a lung fill with inflammatory cells and secretion. Gas exchange is not possible and oxygen level in the blood drops. An individual with pneumonia is feverish; breathing is rapid and shallow; and there is a cough with the production of scanty, rust-coloured sputum. The lips may have a bluish tinge and a sharp pain may be felt at a certain spot on the chest with each inspiration (pleurisy). In severe cases, a person may become confused and very short of breath.

Pneumonia in previously healthy individuals is due to bacterial or viral infection. The administration of an antibiotic such as amoxycillin is the cornerstone of treatment, and should be started as soon as possible. If the organism is sensitive to the antibiotic, improvement is usually rapid. Nevertheless, steps should be taken to secure expert medical help as complications can occur. Patients with pneumonia feel more comfortable propped up on pillows, and paracetamol or aspirin will lower temperature and relieve pain. In severe cases, oxygen should be provided. Inhaled from a cylinder through a mask, this may be life-saving during transit to hospital.

POISONING

Poisoning may be accidental, suicidal or homicidal. Children under the age of four are liable to taste and eat whatever they encounter in the course of exploratory play, and may be poisoned if toxic substances are not kept out of their reach. Adults may mistake a bottle or container of a poisonous substance for something drinkable. This usually occurs when lighting is poor or reading glasses have been misplaced.

The symptoms and signs of poisoning depend very much on the substance and quantity ingested. Thus, every effort should be made to obtain this information. Specific antidotes exist for relatively few of the vast number of potentially poisonous substances available. Treatment, in most cases, is directed towards eliminating the toxic substance and sustaining the vital functions of respiration and circulation. The following steps should be taken:

■ Check breathing and the colour of the tongue and the inside of the lips. If the victim is unconscious, it may be necessary to reposition the head to ensure an unobstructed airway. If breathing is or becomes shallow and very slow, and the patient's tongue and lips become blue, artificial ventilation must be instituted.

■ Feel the pulse. If this is rapid and feeble, the patient is likely to be in shock. If feasible, an intravenous drip should be set up. Certain poisons cause a marked slowing and/or irregularity of the pulse. This is a serious sign.

■ Establish the level of consciousness.

■ If the victim is conscious, and the substance ingested is neither corrosive nor a petrochemical (for example, paraffin), vomiting should be induced. This can be achieved by thrusting two fingers down the person's throat. Drinking a strong solution of mustard and water will also induce vomiting.

Drinking a strong salt solution is inadvisable as salt poisoning can occur. In hospital vomiting is induced by giving the patient an emetic substance known as syrup of ipecacuanha. A stomach wash out may also be performed. This should not be attempted in the field. When vomiting is complete, a drink of milk should be given.

Individuals who have ingested a corrosive substance should be given milk as soon as possible as this will, to some extent, neutralize the corrosive effect of the poison.

■ If the toxic substance is known, and there is access to a telephone or radio, contact a Poisons Information Centre for advice. The container and residual contents (or samples of fruits, berries or plants thought to be responsible) should be taken to hospital with the patient.

■ Transfer the victim to hospital for further treatment and a period of observation.

See also **Artificial Respiration, Food Poisoning, Poisonous Plants, Shock**

Poisonous plants

Some 22 000 species of indigenous plants have been identified in southern Africa. Many hundreds of these are known to contain chemical substances which are toxic to humans and to animals. Plant toxins produce a variety of symptoms and disorders. These include severe skin reactions, irritation and swelling of the mouth and throat, nausea, vomiting, stomach cramps and diarrhoea, progressive liver failure, irregularity of the heartbeat, muscle weakness, mental confusion, convulsions and coma.

It is not possible to list and provide details of even the most common poisonous plants in this book, but it is sound policy not to eat any part of a plant (root, bulb, leaves, fruit) unless it has been positively identified as a

syringa

death cap

fly agaric

castor oil bush

species free of toxins. Particular care should be exercised in ensuring that only edible mushrooms are eaten. When symptoms of poisoning follow the ingestion of plant material, efforts should be made to obtain a sample for identification purposes. Few plant poisons have specific antidotes and the treatment of symptoms is along general lines.

See also **Poisoning**

common thorn apple

PREGNANCY

During the first three months of pregnancy, the circulating blood volume increases by about 25%. This may lead to some reduction in effort tolerance and shortness of breath on exertion. Hormonal changes may cause nausea, particularly on waking (morning sickness). Climbing, trail walking and swimming during the first half of a pregnancy will not cause any harm provided the woman is in good health and avoids extreme exertion.

During the second half of pregnancy, mobility becomes increasingly restricted by the enlarging womb. It is inadvisable to go on expeditions or long walks during this period.

Miscarriage (spontaneous abortion) occurs in many instances because the foetus is severely malformed or otherwise defective. It may also follow serious injury to the mother, or be brought on by severe infection with high fever.

Symptoms of miscarriage include backache, colicky abdominal pains and vaginal bleeding. These will subside once the womb has expelled its contents. Serious haemorrhage may occur if expulsion is incomplete. A woman with the symptoms of miscarriage should be kept at rest. Some pain relief may be obtained with paracetamol or codeine. If the miscarriage is incomplete and haemorrhage continues transfer to hospital is essential.

An ectopic pregnancy occurs when the fertilized egg is implanted in one of the Fallopian tubes, rather than in the wall of the womb. During the first or second month of pregnancy the tube ruptures, often with severe haemorrhage. The woman will usually have missed a period and will experience sudden severe lower abdominal pain, and become faint and weak. She will appear pale and shocked, and have a rapid, feeble pulse. This condition constitutes an emergency as internal haemorrhage can be fatal. Urgent transfer to hospital is essential. If feasible, an intravenous infusion should be set up. Codeine will provide some pain relief.

See also **Bleeding, Shock**

Pulse and Breathing

The rate and strength of a person's pulse will provide a good measure of the state of the heart and circulation. In a healthy state, the pulse can be felt easily on the outer (thumb) aspect of the wrist. In shocked or collapsed individuals, however, the pulse may be

detected only in the neck. The resting pulse rate is determined by state of health and fitness. Those in good athletic training may have resting pulse rates below 60 beats per minute. An increase in pulse rate above 90 beats per minute is brought about by exertion, anxiety, fever, infections, dehydration, hyperthermia, blood loss, shock and heart failure. A very slow pulse – below 50 – is found with hypothermia and heart disorders.

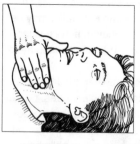

The strength of the pulse is influenced by the force of the heart beat and the volume of circulating blood. It is strong in a feverish individual, and weak and feeble in someone who has fainted, lost a lot of

blood, become dehydrated or is in shock. A return
to normal pulse rate and an increase in strength
are signs of response to treatment, and a general
improvement in well-being.

In normal health, respiration varies between 10
and 20 breaths per minute. Children under the age of
four breathe at a slightly faster rate. The rate slows
during sleep and is increased by effort and anxiety.
Rapid, shallow breathing occurs with fever, pneumonia, chest injury (pneumothorax) and heart failure.
Deep sighing breathing occurs after poisoning with
certain toxins (for example aspirin overdose), and in
liver and kidney failure. A return to normal respiratory
rate usually correlates with improvement in condition.

Pyelitis and Cystitis

Infection of the urinary tract is more common in
females than in males. The individual feels unwell
and may be feverish. There is dull pain in the small of
the back, radiating round to the groin. Urine is
passed frequently and causes burning discomfort.
The urine looks cloudy, often contains blood, and
may have an offensive odour. Antibiotic treatment is
necessary, accompanied by increased fluid intake to
ensure good flow of dilute urine. An individual who
has had an episode of pyelitis or cystitis should consult a doctor, as further investigation and treatment
may be necessary to prevent the condition recurring.

Rabies

Rabies is caused by a virus which is endemic in
meerkats, bats, rats and some other small mammals.
Dogs and monkeys may also become infected. A bite
from any one of these animals can transmit the disease to human beings. The incubation period varies

from 10 days to 6 months. The virus causes inflammation of the brain (encephalitis). Initial symptoms are fever, headache and agitation, followed by intense spasm of the swallowing muscles whenever anything is taken by mouth. The illness progresses through violent mental derangement and convulsions, to coma and death.

As rabies is invariably fatal, active steps must be taken to prevent those bitten by suspect animals from developing the condition. Bite wounds should be thoroughly washed and cleansed with a soap solution, cetrimide or iodine. Suturing should be delayed until there is certainty that no local infection is present. As soon as possible after being bitten, the victim should receive an injection of human rabies immune antibody (gammaglobulin). This should be followed by doses of anti-rabies vaccine, repeated at increasing intervals over a period of three months.

SCORPION STINGS

Scorpions are encountered all over southern Africa. They are found under stones, among dry wood, in the bark of trees and in sandy soil. The sting of a scorpion produces very severe, needle-like pain, which may persist for some hours. It is important to distinguish dangerous scorpions from those whose

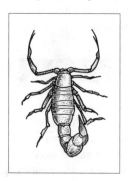

venom produces only minor local reactions. The Buthid family of scorpions produce a powerful neurotoxin which can cause generalized weakness followed by respiratory paralysis and death in children. Buthids are recognized by their small, thin pincers and large, thick tails.

The toxicity of Buthid venom varies with the species – parabuthus being the most powerful. Other, less harmful, scorpion families have well-developed, prominent pincers and thin tails.

Immediate local pain relief from a scorpion sting can be achieved by applying an ice pack. Every attempt should be made to catch and identify the offending scorpion. If it is clearly a non-Buthid, further treatment is unnecessary.

Individuals stung by a Buthid should be kept under careful observation for at least 12 hours. Transfer to hospital may be wise. It is recommended that children under 12 years be given an intramuscular injection of scorpion antivenom. This should also be given to those over 12 years if there is any onset of weakness. Increasing respiratory difficulty calls for artificial ventilation until the patient can be put on to a respirator.

See also **Artificial Respiration**

SHARK ATTACK

Sharks have rows of sharp, pointed teeth with which they are able to inflict terrible injuries. Amputation of limbs, extensive tissue destruction and loss, and massive haemorrhage are the consequences of a shark attack. Death from blood loss and shock is usual unless vigorous resuscitation is started immediately. This should be instituted on the beach or at the riverside, as shock is aggravated by movement and the victim is likely to die during transfer to hospital. Haemorrhage must be arrested by applying direct pressure with pads or cloths over the bleeding areas. The individual should be placed in a horizontal position with the legs slightly elevated.

An intravenous infusion should be set up as soon as possible and allowed to run freely. A strong pain-

killer injection should be administered. If respiration
fails, artificial ventilation should be commenced.
The victim should be transferred to hospital *only*
when there has been effective fluid replacement,
the pain-killer is working well and there is a good,
steady pulse.

See also **Amputation, Bleeding, Shock**

Shock

In its medical sense, the word 'shock' means failure
of the heart and arterial system to meet the body's
requirements for blood circulation. Common causes
of shock include significant blood loss, either exter-
nally or internally, severe dehydration, extensive
burns, heart damage following a heart attack, spinal
cord injury and massive proliferation of bacteria in
the blood stream. Sustained severe pain can cause
and aggravate shock.

The signs of shock are faintness, pallor, visible
sweating, cold clammy skin, rapid weak pulse, and
sighing respiration. If the process is not reversed, the
individual will lose consciousness and, shortly thereafter, heartbeat and respiration will cease.

The first treatment priority is to stop external
bleeding. This is done by applying direct pressure
over the bleeding vessels. Keep the victim warm, and
in a horizontal position with the legs elevated. If there
is pain, administer the strongest pain-killer available
and keep movement to a minimum. If feasible, set up
an intravenous infusion. If severe infection is suspected antibiotic treatment should be instituted. Oral
rehydration fluid and other fluids (though not alcohol)
may be given to the conscious patient. If respiration
ceases, start artificial ventilation and, if necessary,
external cardiac compression. Arrange urgent transfer to hospital.

SLIPPED DISC

The spinal column is composed of bones called vertebrae. Each vertebra consists of a body and a vertebral arch. The vertebral bodies rest one on top of the other and, in the upright position, support the trunk and head. Together, the vertebral arches form the spinal canal which carries the spinal cord. Vertebral bodies are separated from each other by a plate of tough cartilage known as an intervertebral disc.

During strenuous effort, particularly lifting heavy objects with the back bent, part of a disc may be forced out of its natural position. It may then press against the nerves which arise from the spinal cord and leave the spinal canal through openings between the vertebral arches. Slipped disc is most likely to occur in the lower back region, but can also occur in the neck. There is initial acute backache, followed by stiffness, limitation of movement, and pain which radiates down the back of the leg to the heel (or in the case of a neck lesion, down an arm). Pain may be aggravated by coughing or sneezing.

Back injury and slipped disc can be avoided by exercising care when lifting heavy objects. Do not bend over with the spine curved. Adopt a squatting position next to the object to be lifted and then raise it by straightening your knees without bending the spine. Never attempt to lift something which is clearly too heavy for one person to move. An individual with a slipped disc should be kept at rest on a mattress or other firm surface until the symptoms subside. Paracetamol or codeine will provide pain relief. Travel should be avoided, particularly over bumpy roads. The majority of cases respond within a week or two to rest, and surgery is required only when the problem becomes recurrent or chronic.

See also **Back and Neck Injuries**

SMOKE INHALATION

Individuals trapped by a bush fire may suffer from smoke inhalation as well as burns. Injury through smoke inhalation may also be sustained in hut and vehicle fires. Carbon monoxide poisoning occurs when coal and coke-burning braziers are used to heat poorly ventilated and confined spaces.

Smoke inhalation can lead to thermal injury, chemical injury, asphyxia, and carbon monoxide poisoning. The lungs are largely protected from thermal injury by reflex closure of the vocal cords. However, the lips, mouth and nasal cavities, back of the throat and voicebox (larynx) above the vocal cords, may suffer severe burns with rapid development of swelling and airway obstruction.

Chemical injury to the lungs is caused by inhalation of various toxic products of combustion. These cause swelling of bronchial (air) tube linings and constriction of the tubes themselves. This is followed by collections of fluid within the air chambers (alveoli) and pneumonia.

Asphyxia (lack of oxygen) is due to the rapid consumption of oxygen by the fire itself. Insufficient oxygen is left in the air inhaled to sustain life. Carbon monoxide is produced by incomplete combustion of carbon-containing compounds. When inhaled it displaces oxygen from the haemoglobin in red blood cells and leads to oxygen starvation of the tissues.

An individual suffering from severe smoke inhalation will show swelling of the lips, tongue and inside of the throat, while breathing will be noisy and increasingly difficult. Asphyxia and carbon monoxide poisoning cause unconsciousness, irregularity of the heartbeat and fluid congestion of the lungs.

The first priority is to get the victim away from the fire or confined space and into fresh air. If there is evidence of increasing upper airway obstruction, efforts must be made to by-pass the swelling by inserting a needle or small tube into the windpipe (*see* Choking). Artificial ventilation must be instituted if there is respiratory arrest. The most effective treatment for carbon monoxide poisoning is the inhalation of 100% oxygen, and efforts should be made to obtain an oxygen cylinder for use during transfer to hospital. Further treatment may be necessary in the intensive care unit of a hospital.

See also **Artificial Respiration, Asphyxiation, Burns and Scalds, Heart Attack, Shock**

Snake bite

Snake bite is probably the calamity most feared by hikers, climbers and members of expeditions to remote places. In fact, snake bite is uncommon and fatalities are extremely rare. Most snakes move away when they become aware of approaching humans, and are aggressive only when surprised and threatened. An exception is the puff adder which remains still and relies on its markings for camouflage; if stepped upon, it will bite.

Encounters with snakes can be avoided by keeping a sharp look-out when moving through long grass and forests, stepping over logs and rocks, and climbing along mountain ledges. Some protection from bites can be achieved by wearing sturdy boots and thick socks.

The most dangerous venomous snakes found in southern Africa are the puff adder, the cobra, the rinkhals and the mamba. The effects of berg adder venom and boomslang venom are less serious

puff adder

cobra

berg adder

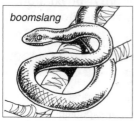

boomslang

mamba

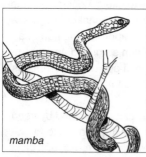

rinkhals

but nevertheless significant. The venom of the puff adder causes extensive local tissue damage and destruction in the vicinity of the bite. Local swelling occurs within minutes, and this is followed over the next 24 hours by discolouration, blistering and the spread of inflammation to the whole limb. The cobra and the mamba produce a neurotoxic venom, which, if injected, causes drooping of the eyelids, poor vision, slurred speech and impaired swallowing followed by respiratory paralysis and death. The venom of the rinkhals and other spitting cobras causes severe inflammation in the eyes but has no serious effect on intact skin. The berg adder also produces a neurotoxin which causes paralysis of the eyelids, eyes and palate. It is not potent enough to paralyse respiration. Effects wear off after several days. Boomslang venom causes destruction of blood elements and spontaneous bleeding which persists for a number of days and can be fatal if not treated with a blood transfusion and a special antivenom.

The effect of a snake bite will depend on the quantity of venom injected. If the snake fails to release venom, the victim will suffer only the local wound. When venom *is* injected, it acts relatively slowly and there is no need to panic. The individual should be kept at rest. Movement will increase blood circulation and therefore the rate at which the venom is absorbed into the bloodstream. A pad should be placed over the wound and firmly bandaged. These two steps will limit the spread of the toxin. The bite area should *not* be cut, squeezed or sucked and a tourniquet should not be used as it is usually ineffective and may lead to gangrene of the limb. Arrange transportation to hospital while checking for signs of developing weakness and respiratory difficulty. If these become severe, artificial ventilation should be started and maintained until the patient can be placed on a respirator. Breathing paralysis can last from 12 to 20 hours after cobra bites, and up to a week after mamba bites. However, a full recovery is usual if adequate ventilation can be sustained. When rinkhals venom enters the eye it should be irrigated as soon as possible using several cups of water.

Antivenom injections undoubtedly counteract the severe effects of snake bite. However, severe and even fatal allergic reactions are possible, and the potency of antivenom that has not been kept in a fridge is suspect. Intravenous administration of snake antivenom is best left to those with special training in its use.

See also **Artificial Respiration, Shock**

Spiders

Spider bites can be painful and may lead to trouble-some, secondary skin infections. There are four species of spider in southern Africa which produce more serious symptoms:

button spider

BUTTON SPIDER
The black button spider has a characteristic bright red streak or spot on the upper surface of the abdomen. There are no markings on the underside of the abdomen. Venom causes muscle pain which spreads rapidly to the limbs, abdomen and chest. There is profuse sweating and a tingling sensation in the skin, with tremor of the limbs and tenseness of the abdominal wall. Respiratory paralysis and cardiac arrest may follow. The brown button spider has a reddish hour-glass shape on the underside of its abdomen. Its venom is less toxic than the black button spider, but may cause serious illness in children.

sac spider

SAC SPIDER
The sac spider is straw-coloured, has long slender legs and large jet-black head appendages. Its venom causes a boil-like lesion at the site of the bite, with considerable local swelling.

VIOLIN SPIDER

This nocturnal spider is brown in colour. The name comes from a violin-shaped marking on the upper surface of the thorax. Bites are initially painless,

violin spider

but later there is intense local reaction with death of tissue, ulceration, severe pain and often unsightly scarring.

SIX-EYED CRAB SPIDER

This reddish-brown spider lives in sand. Bites induce localized swelling and bleeding into the tissues.

The site of a spider bite should be

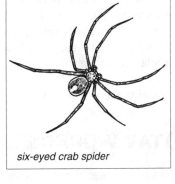
six-eyed crab spider

washed with an antiseptic solution and covered with mercurochrome or antiseptic ointment. Paracetamol will assist pain relief. Spider antiserum is required for the effective treatment of button spider bites, and efforts should be made to obtain a supply from a hospital as quickly as possible. If respiratory paralysis develops, artificial ventilation must be instituted. The bites of the sac spider, the violin spider and the crab spider require local treatment with antiseptic cream and dressings. An antibiotic should be given if secondary infection is suspected.

See also **Artificial Respiration**

SPRAINS AND STRAINS

The term 'sprain' is used when a joint has been wrenched and the surrounding ligaments stretched and damaged. The ankle is the joint most often sprained and thereafter the wrist, the knee and the shoulder. A sprained joint is swollen, tender, and movement is severely restricted by pain.

The term 'strain' is used when a muscle has been overstretched or overexerted resulting in the rupture of some muscle fibres. The belly of the muscle is tender to touch and pain is felt when the muscle is used. Muscle tendons may also be strained.

Rest is the treatment for both sprains and strains. A crêpe bandage will provide support, and pain relief can be obtained with codeine or paracetamol. Swelling should subside after a few days and full function return within a week.

See also Ankle Injuries

STAB WOUNDS

The seriousness of a stab wound depends on the site, the nature of the implement used, and the depth to which it penetrates.

Stab wounds to the head and neck may penetrate the brain, destroy an eye, open the windpipe and/or cause serious bleeding. Chest wounds will be fatal if the heart or major blood vessels are punctured. Entry into a lung can cause the dangerous condition of tension pneumothorax (*see* Chest Injuries).

Stab wounds in the abdomen are associated with stomach and intestinal perforations, damage to the liver, spleen or kidneys, and major bleeding. Limb wounds may involve large blood vessels, nerves and muscle tendons.

The first priority when treating a stab wound is to staunch bleeding. When the vessel is accessible, this can be achieved by sustained direct pressure. Internal haemorrhage is more difficult to control.

The casualty should be placed in a horizontal position with the legs raised above the level of the trunk. An implement still in the wound should not be removed. If feasible, a drip should be set up and allowed to run rapidly.

Stab wounds are almost always inflicted with implements which are not sterile or clean, and infection is a common sequel. Urgent transfer to hospital is advisable for all but the most superficial wounds, as it is always difficult to determine the extent of underlying damage.

See also **Abdominal Injuries, Bleeding, Chest Injuries, Head Injuries, Shock**

STROKE

'Stroke' refers to the sudden bursting or blocking of a blood vessel in the brain. This may cause partial or complete loss of consciousness, and temporary or permanent paralysis of part of the body. If a major blood vessel bursts, the individual will experience sudden, very severe headache, and possible stiffness of the neck. Coma and death may follow.
A blocked blood vessel may cause a period of confusion and disorientation, with loss of memory. Other consequences depend on the part of the brain affected, and the extent of the damage. There may be total loss of power in the arm and leg on one side or just a temporary degree of clumsiness. Speech may be completely lost for a while or just become 'thick' and difficult to follow. Some individuals are left permanently handicapped after a stroke while others recover completely.

Treatment is determined by general condition. The victim who is unconscious requires attention to the airway and should be placed in a horizontal position, with the head elevated slightly above the feet. A conscious person should be kept at rest, comforted and reassured. An aspirin may be administered if this is available. Transfer to hospital should be arranged for further specialist attention.

$\int$ UNBURN

The ultraviolet wavelengths (290–400µu) of sunlight penetrate the skin and can cause an inflammatory reaction varying from a slight 'blush' to very painful redness, with swelling and blistering. The severity of the reaction is directly related to the duration of sun exposure and inversely to the amount of natural pigment (melanin) in the individual's skin.

Recurrent sunburn over a number of years induces permanent damage to elastic and other supporting tissue in the skin. It also leads to the production of abnormal cells which, in time, can give rise to skin cancers. These are many times more common in white-skinned people who live in southern Africa and Australia than in the sun-starved populations of northern Europe.

Prevent sunburn by applying sun-tan lotion or blockout to sun-exposed parts of the body *before going outside.* Special attention should be given to the face, back of the neck, upper chest, backs of hands and behind the knees if wearing shorts. Always wear a hat in sunny weather to protect the face and neck. Consider walking in a light-weight, long-sleeved shirt, and just-above-the-knee shorts, as this will reduce the skin area exposed to the sun. Check that babies and children are adequately protected against sunburn. When severe sunburn *has* occurred some relief can be obtained by applying cold water compresses and soothing lotions. Pain and discomfort can be eased with paracetamol or codeine. Further sun exposure should be avoided until the skin is healing well.

See also **Heat Stroke**

TICK-BITE FEVER

Ticks are found in bush and long grass. They attach themselves to the legs and bodies of passing animals and humans.

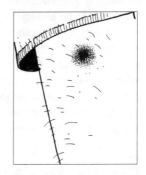

Tick-bite fever develops one week after being bitten by a tick infected with organisms called rickettsia. The initial symptoms are fever, severe headache, and marked sensitivity to bright light. An ulcer with a hard black centre can be found on the skin at the site of the bite. Glands in the area may be swollen, and a reddish rash appears on the trunk and limbs. This rash is often

prominent on the palms of the hands. Pneumonia and heart inflammation are possible complications.

The victim of tick-bite fever should be kept at rest in subdued light. Codeine or paracetamol will provide some relief from headache. The condition responds rapidly to treatment, with either tetracycline or erythromycin, and every effort should be made to obtain one of these antibiotics.

TOOTHACHE AND TOOTH INJURIES

Individuals about to embark on a long climbing trip or other extended expedition are advised to visit a dentist before leaving home, and undergo any dental treatment necessary. Chronic toothache can be very debilitating. It is inadvisable for an unskilled person to attempt tooth extraction without the appropriate instruments. Some pain-relief can be obtained with paracetamol or codeine. Teeth may break when a very hard object is bitten or there is severe facial injury. When the jaw is fractured, teeth may become malaligned. Loose fragments should be removed from the mouth but the root sections left in place as a basis for tooth reconstruction at a later stage.

TRAVEL SICKNESS

This is also called motion sickness, car sickness or sea sickness. Susceptible individuals develop abdominal discomfort and nausea in moving vehicles, aeroplanes and on boats. These symptoms are accompanied by sweating, rapid heart beat, and a general feeling of distress; vomiting often follows. Travel sickness is due to excessive and repetitive stimulation of the balance organs (labyrinths) by the motion of the vehicle. Symptoms resolve spontaneously and completely within 30 minutes of leaving the vehicle.

Susceptibility to travel sickness varies widely, and factors like anxiety, fatigue and hunger may influence its development. Individuals who are prone to car sickness should, if possible, travel in the front seat and keep their eyes on the road. Sucking barley sugar or boiled sweets is found helpful by some.

A number of drugs are effective in preventing motion sickness, and the highly susceptible individual should take one of these before embarking on a long journey. Unfortunately, drowsiness is a common side-effect of these drugs.

*T*YPHOID

Typhoid fever is a disease which affects the digestive tract. It is caused by Salmonella typhi, an organism found in water contaminated with excreta from infected persons. Hence the importance of boiling or otherwise treating all drinking water obtained from suspect sources. Typhoid may also be passed on by food handlers who have become carriers — someone who has apparently recovered completely from typhoid but continues to excrete organisms in the faeces. This is usually because of persisting infection in the gall bladder. A carrier should be excluded from food handling and preparation until proved free of typhoid organisms. The incubation period for typhoid, after drinking contaminated water, is usually about 10 days, but may be much longer. The victim may have travelled a considerable distance from the source of infection before the first symptoms appear. The illness has a gradual onset with headache, fever and abdominal discomfort. Cough and bronchitis are common, and a rash of red spots sometimes can be seen on the abdomen. Untreated, the patient may suffer massive bowel haemorrhage and intestinal perforation. This is often fatal.

Typhoid is a serious disease which caused more deaths during the Anglo-Boer War than did the actual hostilities. Today, it is treated with specific antibiotics and deaths are infrequent. Careful nursing is nevertheless necessary, and a person who develops symptoms suggestive of typhoid should be taken to hospital without delay.

UNCONSIOUSNESS

A conscious individual is fully aware of all that is going on around him or her, and will be able to respond to questions with rational answers, and retain memories of events taking place. Impaired consciousness varies in degree from a state of mild disorientation and confusion to profound unresponsive coma. In hospitals, it is traditional to grade levels of consciousness according to the *Glasgow Coma Scale*. On this scale, the fully conscious individual scores 15 and the totally unresponsive scores 3. A change in the score reflects improvement or deterioration in the level of consciousness.

There are many causes of impaired consciousness: choking, near drowning, electric shock, head injury, hyperthermia, hypothermia, poisoning (including alcohol poisoning) and inhalation of toxic fumes. Disease processes include diabetes mellitus, epilepsy, stroke and severe lack of oxygen as a result of pneumonia or asthma. There may also be loss of consciousness in states of profound shock and dehydration, and following an anaphylactic response to a bee sting.

The first aid care of an unconscious person must be directed towards the maintenance of an open airway and the support of blood circulation. The individual should be placed in a supine position or on one side. The head must be positioned so that the chin is elevated. Check that the mouth is empty. If the pulse is rapid and weak, an intravenous infusion should be set up (if possible). An unconscious person must not be given fluid or any other substance by mouth. If respiration fails, artificial ventilation must be instituted and if the heart beat ceases, external cardiac massage must be started. Specific treatment will depend on the underlying condition causing unconsciousness.

Recovery positions

GLASGOW COMA SCALE

Response	Score
Eye opening	
Spontaneous	4
To verbal command	3
To pain	2
No response	1
Best motor response	
Obeys commands	6
Localizes pain	5
Flexion withdrawal	4
Flexion posturing	3
Extension posturing	2
No response	1
Best verbal response	
Oriented, converses	5
Disoriented, converses	4
Inappropriate words	3
Incomprehensible sounds	2
No response	1

See also **Artificial Respiration, Heart Attack**

VERTIGO

Vertigo is a feeling of rotation – either of the individual's own body or of the surroundings. The sensation is often accompanied by nausea and vomiting, and the individual may have difficulty in standing upright and walking. Vertigo is caused by dysfunction of the balance apparatus which forms part of the inner ear. This may be due to direct spread of infection from the middle ear chamber or to virus infection in the bloodstream. Vertigo may also be a symptom of serious brain disease and may follow a stroke. It is not uncommon among hysterical subjects. Sensitive individuals may experience a sensation of unsteadiness when looking down from the top of a high rock-face or cliff. This subjective experience is not true vertigo.

An individual with vertigo is usually least distressed when in a horizontal position. Some relief is obtained with anti-motion sickness drugs (*see* Travel Sickness). If there is obvious ear infection, an antibiotic should be administered; vertigo due to infection will usually subside within a few days to a week. Persistent vertigo suggests a serious underlying cause and in these cases, specialist investigation is necessary.

VOMITING

Vomiting, the forceful expulsion of stomach contents, is a symptom of an underlying disorder. There are many causes. It is common for children with infections in the ears, throat or chest, to vomit during the initial stages of the illness. Meningitis (inflammation of the membranes surrounding the brain) causes vomiting, severe headache and fever. Vomiting is an early symptom of food poisoning and gastro-enteritis; it occurs when there is raised intracranial pressure after head injury, and follows the ingestion of certain poisonous substances. Excessive alcohol intake is a recognized cause, as is a bumpy ride in a boat, aeroplane or car. Vomiting often occurs in the early stages of appendicitis, and is a prominent feature of intestinal obstruction when it occurs in association with severe colicky abdominal pain and total constipation.

Vomitus usually consists of recently ingested foodstuffs and gastric secretion. Fresh blood in the vomitus, if not from a recent nose bleed, may indicate bleeding from a stomach or duodenal ulcer, or dilated veins at the lower end of the oesophagus.

To treat vomiting one must treat the underlying condition. In general, solid foods should not be taken for several hours; small sips of water or rehydration fluid will usually be tolerated. If vomiting is profound and signs of dehydration develop, an intravenous infusion should be set up. When other symptoms and signs suggest meningitis, raised intracranial pressure, or serious intra-abdominal disease, rapid transfer to hospital is essential.

See also **Dehydration**

USEFUL ADDRESSES

Government Printer (for maps)
Private Bag X 85, Bosman Street, Pretoria 0001

Hiking Federation of South Africa
Head Office, PO Box 1420, Randburg 2125
Tel: (011) 8866524 or 8866507
Fax: (011) 8866013

Mountain Club of South Africa
Cape Town: 97 Hatfield Street, Cape Town 8001
Tel: (021) 453412
Tygerberg: PO Box 2125, Bellville 7535
Stellenbosch: PO Box 152, Stellenbosch 7600
Hottentots Holland: PO Box 1100,
Somerset West 7130
Paarl/Wellington: PO Box 2645, Paarl 7620
Worcester: PO Box 373, Worcester 6850
Eastern Province: PO Box 1274, Port Elizabeth 6000
Orange Free State: PO Box 1291, Bloemfontein 9300
Natal: PO Box 4535, Durban 4000
Northern Natal: PO Box 1362, Newcastle 2940
Transvaal: PO Box 1641, Houghton 2041
Northern Transvaal: PO Box 1418, Pretoria 0001
National Hiking Way Board
Private Bag X93, Pretoria 0001
Tel: (012) 3103839
Fax: (012) 3200949

National Parks Board
PO Box 787, Pretoria 0001
Tel: (012) 3431991
Fax: (012) 3430905
PO Box 7400, Roggebaai 8012
Tel: (021) 222810
Fax: (021) 246211

St John Ambulance
19 Woolston Road, Westcliffe, Johannesburg 2001
Tel: (011) 6465520

POISON CENTRES

PWV
Poisons Information Centre, Johannesburg
General Hospital
Tel: (011) 6422417 or (011) 4883108
Medical Rescue International
Tel: (011) 4037080
Arwyp Emergency Services, Hydromed Hospital
Tel: 0800 091911 (toll free) or (011) 9221145

Western Cape
Pharmacology and Toxicology Consultation Centre,
Tygerberg Hospital
Tel: (021) 9316129 or (021) 9386235
Poisons Reference Service, Red Cross War Memorial
Children's Hospital
Tel: (021) 6895227
Emergency Unit, Groote Schuur Hospital
Tel: (021) 4044450

Eastern Cape
Livingstone Hospital Intensive Care Unit
(Mon.-Fri.: 08h00-16h30)
Tel: (041) 4052455
Provincial Hospital, Drug Information Centre,
Port Elizabeth
(Mon.-Fri.: 07h45-16h15; Sat.: 08h00-11h45)
Tel: (041) 3923220
Department of Paediatrics, Frere Hospital
Tel: (0431) 491077 (office hours); (0431) 491118 or
(0431) 491111 (after hours)
Paediatric Intensive Care Unit, Cecilia Makiwane
Hospital, Mdantsane
Tel: (0403) 613111 or (0403) 613121

KwaZulu/Natal
St Augustine's Trauma and Poison Unit, Durban
Tel: 0800 333444 (toll free) or (031) 211221

FURTHER READING

Branch, B. *Field Guide to the Snakes and Other Reptiles of Southern Africa*, Struik, Cape Town 1992

Bristow, D. *Best Hikes in Southern Africa*, Struik, Cape Town 1992

Filmer, M. *South African Spiders: An Identification Guide*, Struik, Cape Town 1993

Holm, M. *Insects*, Struik, Cape Town 1993

Levy, J. *Complete Guide to Walks and Trails in Southern Africa*, Struik, Cape Town 1993

Moll, E. & G. *Poisonous Plants*, Struik, Cape Town 1993

Newlands, G. *Spiders*, Struik, Cape Town 1993

Newlands, G. *Venomous Creatures*, Struik, Cape Town 1993

Patterson, R. *Snakes*, Struik, Cape Town 1993

Stevens, U. *The South African Backpacker's Cookbook*, Struik, Cape Town 1992

The British Red Cross Society *South African Practical First Aid*, Struik, Cape Town 1993

The St John Ambulance Association and Brigade, authorised manual of the St John Ambulance and Red Cross Society, *The South African First Aid Manual*, Struik, Cape Town 1993

Van Eeden, J., comp. and ed. *The South African Mountain Leadership Guide*, Mountain Club of South Africa (Northern Transvaal section) 1991

INDEX

A

abdominal injuries 44
accident, how to handle
   an 14-5
allergic reactions 44-5
amputation 45-5
animal bites 46:
ankle injuries 47
appendicitis 48
artificial respiration 49-51
asphyxiation 51
asthma 52

B

back and neck injuries 53-4:
bee stings 55-6
bilharzia 56
bites
   animal 46
   insect 103-4
   snake 123-5
   spider 126-7
bleeding 57-8
blindness 59-60
blisters 60
boils 61
breathing, and pulse 116-7
bruises 61-2
burns and scalds 62-3:

C

camp, setting up 25-9
chest injuries 63-5:
chest pain 65-6
childbirth 66-7:
choking 67-9
clothing 9-10
clothing checklist 10
compass, using a 24
concussion 69
convulsions 70-1

cramp 71
cuts 72
cystitis, pyelitis and 117

D

death 72-3:
dehydration 74-5
diabetes 75-6
diarrhoea 76-7
dislocated joints 77-8
drowning 39, 40
drowning 39, 40, 79
drug overdose 80

E

ear injuries and
   infections 81-2:
electric shock 82-3
epilepsy 83-4
equipment 10-1
equipment checklist 11
examination of an injured
   person 15-7
exhaustion, heat 99-100
eye injuries 84-5

F

face and nose
   injuries 86
fainting 87-8
fever 88-9
   tick-bite 131
finding the way 22-4
fire 34-6
fireplaces 26-7
first aid kits 19-21
food 11-3
food poisoning 89-90
footwear 9
fractures 91-2
frostbite 93-4

G
gastro-enteritis 94-5
Glasgow coma scale 135

H
head injuries 96
heat exhaustion 99-100
hypothermia 100-2
hysteria 102-3

I
improvising shelter 31-2
injured person
  examination of 15-7
  moving 18-9
injuries
  abdominal 44
  ankle 47
  back and neck 53-4
  chest 63-5
  ear 81-2
  eye 84-5
  face and nose 86
  head 96
  tooth 132
insect stings and
  bites 103-4

J
jelly fish and other marine
  creatures 104-6
joints, dislocated 77-8

K
kidney stones 107
kits
  first aid 19-21
  survival 13

l
leadership and morale 21
leeches 107-8
lightning strikes 33

M
malaria 108-9
map reading 22
maps 22
marine creatures, jellyfish
  and other 104-6
menu, sample 12
Metro 15
morale, leadership and 21
mountain safety
  guidelines 29-31
mountain sickness 109-10
moving an injured
  person 18-9

P
party, composition of
  the 6-7, 8
permits 7
planning and preparation 6
planning, route 7-8
plants, poisonous 113-4
pneumonia 110-1
poison centres 140
poisoning 111-3
  food 89-90
poisonous plants 113-4
pregnancy 115-6
pulse 16
pulse and breathing 116-7
pyelitis and cystitis 117

R
rabies 117-8
radio, use of a 41
rescuing a drowning
  person 39-40
river crossing 37-8, 39
route planning 7-8

S
scalds, burns and 62-3
scorpion stings 118-9
setting up camp 25-9